# Scott, Foresman

# Science

## Series Consultant

**Irwin L. Slesnick**
Department of Biology
Western Washington University
Bellingham, Washington

## Program Consultant

**Ronald D. Anderson**
Laboratory for Research
in Science and Mathematics Education
University of Colorado
Boulder, Colorado

## Reading Consultant

**Robert A. Pavlik**
Reading-Language Arts Department
Cardinal Stritch College
Milwaukee, Wisconsin

## Special Writers

Laboratories
**Alfred DeVito**
Science Education
Purdue University
Lafayette, Indiana

Enrichment Features
**David Newton**
Department of Chemistry
Salem State College
Salem, Massachusetts

## Authors

**Michael R. Cohen**
School of Education
Indiana University
Indianapolis, Indiana

**Bette J. Del Giorno**
Science Consultant
Fairfield Public Schools
Fairfield, Connecticut

**Jean Durgin Harlan**
Education Division
University of Wisconsin, Parkside
Kenosha, Wisconsin

**Alan J. McCormack**
Science and Mathematics
Teaching Center
College of Education
University of Wyoming
Laramie, Wyoming

**John R. Staver**
College of Education and
College of Liberal Arts and Sciences
University of Illinois at Chicago
Chicago, Illinois

## Scott, Foresman and Company

Editorial Offices: Glenview, Illinois

Regional Offices: Palo Alto, California
Tucker, Georgia • Glenview, Illinois
Oakland, New Jersey • Dallas, Texas

Cover: Raccoons live mainly in woods and swamps. They are found throughout the United States and southern Canada.

## Reviewers and Contributors

**Gretchen M. Alexander**
Program Coordinator
Museum of Science and Industry
Chicago, Illinois

**Daniel W. Ball**
Division of Education
Northeast Missouri State University
Kirksville, Missouri

**Mary Coban**
Teacher
Divine Savior School
Norridge, Illinois

**Thomas Graika**
Science Chairman
School District 102
LaGrange, Illinois

**Robert G. Guy**
Science Teacher
Big Lake Elementary School
Sedro Woolley, Washington

**Irma G. Hamilton**
Science Teacher
Oglethorpe Elementary School
Atlanta, Georgia

**Judy Haney**
Teacher
East Noble School Corporation
Kendallville, Indiana

**Garth P. Harris**
Teacher
Lincoln Elementary School
Evanston, Illinois

**Edwina Hill**
Principal
Oglethorpe Elementary School
Atlanta, Georgia

**LaVerne Jackson, Sr.**
Science Teacher
Medgar Evers Elementary School
Chicago, Illinois

**Hollis R. Johnson**
Astronomy Department
Indiana University
Bloomington, Indiana

**Irene S. Kantner**
Teacher
Lincoln Elementary School
Evanston, Illinois

**Sol Krasner**
Department of Physics
University of Chicago
Chicago, Illinois

**Dolores Mann**
Teacher
Glenview Public Schools
Glenview, Illinois

**Phillip T. Miyazawa**
Instructional Consultant
Science Education
Denver Public Schools
Denver, Colorado

**Anita E. Moore**
Principal
George Howland Elementary School
Chicago, Illinois

**Janet Ostrander**
Teacher
Indian Trail School
Highland Park, Illinois

**Barbara Scott**
Teacher
Crown Magnet School
Chicago, Illinois

**Elaine R. Seaman**
Teacher
Greenbrier Elementary School
Arlington Heights, Illinois

**R. A. Slotter**
Department of Chemistry
Northwestern University
Evanston, Illinois

**Anita Snell**
Coordinator of Primary Education
Spring Branch Independent
School District
Houston, Texas

**Lois Spangler**
Teacher
Central School
Great Meadows, New Jersey

**Carol Leth Stone**
Biology Writer
Stanford, California

**Johanna F. Strange**
Model Laboratory School
Eastern Kentucky University
Richmond, Kentucky

**William D. Thomas**
Science Supervisor
Escambia County Schools
Pensacola, Florida

**Dorothy Wallinga**
Christian Schools International
Grand Rapids, Michigan

**Les Wallinga**
Science Teacher
Calvin Christian Junior High School
Wyoming, Michigan

ISBN: 0-673-42024-8

Copyright © 1986, Scott, Foresman and Company, Glenview, Illinois. All rights Reserved. Printed in the United States of America.

12345678910–KPK–9493929190898887868 5

# When You Read This Book

**1** Read the questions.

**2** Look at the pictures.

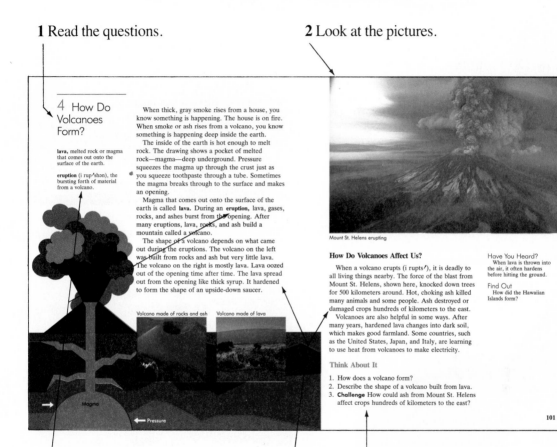

### 4 How Do Volcanoes Form?

**lava,** melted rock or magma that comes out onto the surface of the earth.

**eruption** (i rup′shon), the bursting forth of material from a volcano.

When thick, gray smoke rises from a house, you know something is happening. The house is on fire. When smoke or ash rises from a volcano, you know something is happening deep inside the earth.

The inside of the earth is hot enough to melt rock. The drawing shows a pocket of melted rock—magma—deep underground. Pressure squeezes the magma up through the crust just as you squeeze toothpaste through a tube. Sometimes the magma breaks through to the surface and makes an opening.

Magma that comes out onto the surface of the earth is called **lava.** During an **eruption,** lava, gases, rocks, and ashes burst from the opening. After many eruptions, lava, rocks, and ash build a mountain called a volcano.

The shape of a volcano depends on what came out during the eruptions. The volcano on the left was built from rocks and ash but very little lava. The volcano on the right is mostly lava. Lava oozed out of the opening time after time. The lava spread out from the opening like thick syrup. It hardened to form the shape of an upside-down saucer.

Volcano made of rocks and ash

Volcano made of lava

Magma

Pressure

Mount St. Helens erupting

#### How Do Volcanoes Affect Us?

When a volcano erupts (i rupts′), it is deadly to all living things nearby. The force of the blast from Mount St. Helens, shown here, knocked down trees for 500 kilometers around. Hot, choking ash killed many animals and some people. Ash destroyed or damaged crops hundreds of kilometers to the east.

Volcanoes are also helpful in some ways. After many years, hardened lava changes into dark soil, which makes good farmland. Some countries, such as the United States, Japan, and Italy, are learning to use heat from volcanoes to make electricity.

#### Think About It

1. How does a volcano form?
2. Describe the shape of a volcano built from lava.
3. **Challenge** How could ash from Mount St. Helens affect crops hundreds of kilometers to the east?

Have You Heard?
When lava is thrown into the air, it often hardens before hitting the ground.

Find Out
How did the Hawaiian Islands form?

101

**3** Find the answer.

**5** Use what you learned.

**4** Learn the science words.

# UNIT ONE Animal Life

# UNIT TWO Weather

# UNIT THREE Forces Within the Earth

# UNIT FOUR Changes in the Earth's Surface

# UNIT FIVE Adaptations to Surroundings

# UNIT SIX Work and Energy

# UNIT SEVEN Flowering Plants

# UNIT EIGHT
# Populations and the Environment

# UNIT ONE
# ANIMAL LIFE

It is made
   very delicately,
   every inch counts.
It is their home,
   their food,
   their everything,
a birthplace for a new
   beginning.

Doug Rapp *age 9*

# Chapter 1
# Animal Behavior

Many kinds of animals live around you. They get food, make noises, build homes, and feed their young. But different animals do not do these things in the same ways. You can learn how animals act by looking at them carefully. The rabbit in the picture gets food by eating the young shoots of plants. A fox hunts small animals to eat. Some birds eat nuts and seeds. Other birds catch insects or worms.

The lessons in this chapter will help you understand why different animals act in different ways.

1 Observing How Animals Act

2 What Makes Animals Behave as They Do?

3 How Do Animals Communicate?

4 How Do Some Animals Live in Societies?

# 1 Observing How Animals Act

You can learn how animals act by observing them. Watch fish swim to the top of a tank when you add food. Watch caterpillars eat leaves. If you have a pet, observe the way it acts when you come home from school. Notice what it does when you put out its food. You can watch other animals too.

You can study mealworms like the one in the picture. Place several mealworms in a box. Look at them through a hand lens. Watch how they move. Draw a mealworm. Describe its movements.

Gently touch a mealworm's tail with the eraser end of your pencil. Then, touch its head with the eraser. Describe and record the mealworm's actions.

## Think About It

1. How do mealworms act when they are touched?
2. How many legs does a mealworm have?
3. **Challenge** How could you find out if other animals behave like mealworms?

Mealworm

# 2 What Makes Animals Behave as They Do?

behavior (bi hā′vyər), the way a living thing acts.

behave (bi hāv′), act toward surroundings.

stimulus (stim′yə ləs), anything in the surroundings that brings about a change in behavior. [Plural: stimuli (stim′yə lī).]

response (ri spons′), activity that occurs because of a stimulus.

You do not always act in the same way. If you are hungry, you might look for an apple or other food. After a meal, you would not be likely to look for food. You do not act in the same way in the classroom as you do on the playground.

The way an animal acts is its **behavior.** Different kinds of animals act—or **behave**—differently. A mealworm will usually back away when you touch it. If you touched a pet dog or cat, would it behave the same way?

Something in an animal's surroundings that makes it behave a certain way is a **stimulus.** Touch, light, sound, heat, cold, odor, and food are stimuli. The way an animal behaves because of a stimulus is a **response.** Moving toward or away from a stimulus is a response. Fighting, hiding, hunting for food, building a nest, and caring for young are also responses. The bird in the picture is feeding its young. The wide-open mouths of the young birds are stimuli to the parent bird. The parent's response is to feed the young birds.

Parent bird feeding its young

Insect flying toward a light

A stimulus causes different responses in different kinds of animals. If you shine a light at a mealworm, it might back away. The light is a stimulus. Backing away is the mealworm's response to light. Mealworms hide in dark places. However, the insect in the picture flew *toward* a light. Its response to light is not the same as the response of a mealworm.

An animal's response to a stimulus also depends on the animal's senses. Many animals, such as some kinds of fish, that live all their lives in caves are blind. They cannot have a response to light. Some animals can sense things we cannot sense. Bees see light and colors that we cannot see. Look at the two pictures of a flower. When we look at the flower, it looks like the upper picture. To a bee, it looks like the lower picture. The colors help the bee find the center of the flower. Rattlesnakes sense tiny differences in temperature. This sense helps snakes find the animals they catch for food.

The flower we see

The flower the bee sees

Find Out

Use a reference book to find out a cricket's response to the stimulus of temperature.

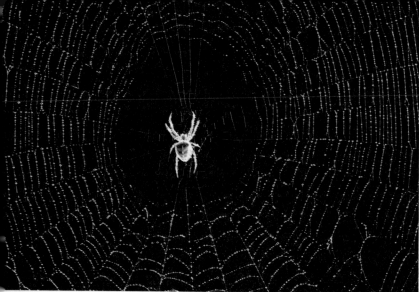

Spider in its web

Baltimore oriole on its nest

instinct (in′stingkt), act an animal does without being taught.

## Are All Responses Learned?

Some of your responses are learned. You learn to say "Thank you" for a gift. Some responses are not learned. You do not need to learn to pull your hand away from a hot stove.

In the same way, some animal responses are learned and some are not. The acts animals do without being taught are **instincts.** This spider was not taught to spin a web. It knew how to spin a web when it came out of its egg. The Baltimore oriole was not taught how to build the nest shown in the picture. The bird knew by instinct how to build a nest. Sparrows know how to sing by instinct. But they learn what notes to sing by listening to other sparrows. A lion cub does not know how to hunt by instinct. Adult lions teach the cubs to hunt.

### Think About It

1. List three ways animals respond to stimuli.
2. How is instinct different from learning?
3. **Challenge** What stimulus might cause a spider to spin a web?

8

# Activity

## Recording Mealworms' Response to Food

**Purpose**

To observe and record mealworms' response to food.

**You Will Need**

- several mealworms
- shoe box
- kitchen timer or clock with a second hand
- bran or cereal flakes

**Directions**

1. Place several mealworms in a shoe box.
2. Observe the mealworms for ten minutes.
3. Record how long they stay in different parts of the box. Use the timer or clock to find out how long the mealworms stay in the middle of the box, along the walls, and up on the sides.
4. Place a pile of bran or cereal flakes in one corner of the box. Observe the mealworms for ten minutes. Record how long they stay in the different parts of the box. Use the timer or clock to time your observations. When you are finished, return your mealworms to their jar.
5. Compare the results from your two observations. Discuss your results with other students.

**Think About It**

1. Were the movements of your mealworms different in the two parts of the activity? If so, how were they different?
2. Did all your classmates get the same results from their mealworms? If not, how were the results different?
3. What was the stimulus in the activity? What were the mealworms' responses?
4. **Challenge** How could you design an experiment to show that mealworms are looking for food, and not just getting out of the light?

# 3 How Do Animals Communicate?

**communicate**
(kə myü′nə kāt), give or receive information that is understood.

You give information to other people when you speak. You get information when you listen to others. You also give and get information without using words. You wave a greeting to a friend. You nod your head to show you agree.

Animals do not speak a language as people do. But they give information—or **communicate**—in other ways. Some animals communicate by making sounds. Each call or cry carries a message. This prairie dog barks to warn other prairie dogs of danger. Other animals communicate by the way they act. The way an animal moves can give a message. The way a bee moves in the hive tells where flowers are found. Some animals give off odors other animals can follow. Many animals find mates by following an odor.

Animals send out and receive many kinds of messages. They can signal that they want food or have found food. They can warn others. They can claim a place as their home or try to get a mate.

Prairie dog

   Dolphins chirp and squeak as they swim. They also make sounds people cannot hear. Some sounds help dolphins find food and locate danger. Some sounds send information to other dolphins.

## How Do Animals Communicate About Food?

   Animals have many ways to communicate about food. When a young robin wants food, it makes peeping sounds. The baby peeps until a parent robin brings it food. When a herring gull finds lots of food, it gives a loud cry to call other gulls. But if it finds only enough food for itself, the gull eats without making a loud cry. An ant that finds food leaves an odor trail as it returns to the nest. The odor tells other ants where to find the food. The ants in the picture are following a trail of odor to some food.

## How Else Do Animals Communicate?

Some animals behave in special ways to attract a mate. A male sparrow's song attracts female sparrows. The peacock in the picture is spreading his brightly colored tail to attract a female.

Some animals warn others when danger is near. A crow makes a cry that warns other crows. Elephants trumpet a warning to others in the herd. The beaver in the picture slaps the water with its strong, broad tail when danger is near.

Animals warn others with sounds or by their behavior. The growls of a lion and the hissing of a snake are warnings. A cat arches its back when it is ready to defend itself. The porcupine in the picture rolled itself into a ball of quills. It is warning other animals to stay away.

### Think About It

1. List two ways animals communicate without sound.
2. How do animals warn others of danger?
3. **Challenge** Explain how you could communicate with a friend without using words.

Beaver

Porcupine

Peacock

# Discover!

## The Dancing Bees

To nectar

A bee lands in a hive and begins dancing around in a figure eight. What is happening? Is the bee sick? No, it is just "talking" to the other bees.

In order for honeybees to make honey, they must use nectar—a sweet liquid from flowers. A group of bees does not spend a lot of time searching for flowers that have nectar. They fly right to the flowers with the nectar.

How do honeybees know where to find the flowers with nectar? For many years, this mystery puzzled scientists who studied bees.

The mystery was solved in the early 1900s by Karl von Frisch, an Austrian scientist. Dr. von Frisch spent many long hours watching the behavior of honeybees. He learned what a bee does when it returns to the hive after finding nectar. First, the bee leaves a drop of nectar in the hive. The odor of the nectar tells other bees what kind of flowers to look for. Then, the bee does one of two dances. A circle dance, such as the one shown, tells the bees that the nectar is less than 100 meters from the hive. With this information, the bees fly around, looking for flowers less than 100 meters away. They depend on sight and smell to find the flowers.

The other kind of dance is done in a figure eight, as shown in the drawing. This dance tells the other bees two things. First, it says the nectar is more than 100 meters from the hive. The dance also tells what direction the bees should fly to find the nectar. The middle line of the figure eight points to where the nectar can be found.

Today, scientists have learned that some bees can find the nectar without watching the dance. They seem to listen to quiet sounds that the bee makes while doing the dance.

We still have many things to learn about the honeybee dances. But, to the other bees, the dance of the honeybee is a language they understand.

# 4 How Do Some Animals Live in Societies?

**society** (sə sī′ə tē), organized community of animals.

**social** (sō′shəl) **insect,** insect that lives in an organized community and has a special job.

People living and working together form a **society.** Some animals live in societies too. Animals in a society can communicate with each other. They do jobs needed by the society, such as warning of danger and caring for young. Honeybees, ants, prairie dogs, wolves, and baboons all live in societies.

## What Are Insect Societies Like?

Insects that live in societies are **social insects.** Most social insects live in a nest or hive. The members of the society have certain jobs. Many social insects know other members of the group by their odors.

More than forty thousand bees can live in a honeybee hive. Termites and ants also live in societies. As many as three million termites can live in a single nest. Army ants do not build a nest that looks like other insect nests. The picture shows the living nest of army ants hooked together by their legs. They hang from tree branches or inside hollow logs. Hornets and some kinds of wasps also live in societies. They make paper by chewing up wood and other plant matter. Then, they use the paper to build nests like the one in the picture.

Hornet's nest

Army ants hooked together in a living nest

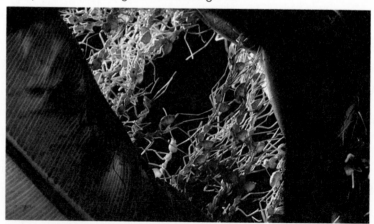

Inside a beehive

Honeybees live in a hive made of cells with wax walls like the ones in the picture. Bees do different jobs in the society. The **queen bee** is a female larger than the other bees. She lays thousands of eggs. Other bees feed and care for her. A hive usually has only one queen at a time. Queens live about five years. The **worker bee** is also a female. Workers do not lay eggs. But they do all the rest of the work in the hive. Workers usually live only about six weeks. The **drone bee** is a male. Drones are about the same size as workers. They do no work around the hive. Their job is to mate with the queen. Drones live about six months. They do not sting.

Worker bees do several different tasks in the hive. They feed and care for the queen and for the young. Workers take honey and other food and feed it to other bees. They help build and repair the cells of the hive. They also defend the hive from enemies. Some workers fly out of the hive to visit flowers. They collect nectar—a sweet liquid bees use to make honey. They store the honey in empty cells in the hive. In winter the bees live on stored food.

**queen bee,** female bee that lays the eggs in a bee hive.

**worker bee,** female bee that does the work for a bee hive.

**drone** (drōn) **bee,** male honeybee.

## Have You Heard?

Some kinds of termites build nests in mounds up to 6 meters high. Termite soldiers have huge heads and very strong jaws. They defend the nest against attack. But they cannot take care of themselves. They must be fed by workers or they will starve.

## What Are Other Animal Societies Like?

Many other kinds of animals live in societies. They work together to care for young, get food, and defend the group. Some members of a group act as guards. They warn the others of danger.

Baboons are monkeys that live in Africa. They spend most of their time on the ground. In a baboon society, the animals share the tasks. Older males protect females and babies. The young male in the picture is acting as a guard. He is watching for danger. If he sees an enemy, he will scream a warning. All the males will join together to fight off the enemy.

### Think About It

1. How can living in a society help animals?
2. Describe the honeybee society.
3. **Challenge** What might happen to a young baboon that left the group?

# Tie It Together

## Sum It Up

On a sheet of paper, write a story about an animal that lives in a society. In your story, answer the following questions about the animal.

1. How will the animal respond to a stimulus, such as light, heat, sound, or odor?

2. How does the animal's response to a stimulus affect the way it lives?

3. How does the animal communicate with other animals? What kind of information does it communicate?

4. What is the animal's job in its society?

5. What jobs do the other animals in the society have?

## Challenge!

1. Design an experiment to find out if mealworms respond to cold without hurting the mealworm.

2. What might happen to an animal that did not respond to a temperature change, light, sound, or touch?

3. A baby duck can swim even if it has never lived with other ducks. Does it know how to swim by instinct or by learning? Why do you think so?

4. What might happen if the animals living in a society could not communicate with each other?

5. What might the tasks be in a termite society? How do you think termites communicate with other termites?

## Science Words

behave

behavior

communicate

drone bee

instinct

queen bee

response

social insect

society

stimulus

worker bee

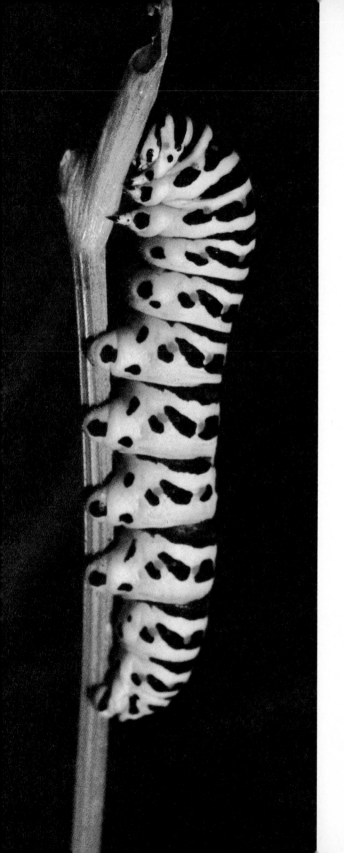

# Chapter 2
# Life Cycles of Animals

Young dogs, cats, fish, and many other animals look much like their parents. But the parents of the caterpillar in the picture were brightly colored butterflies. The caterpillar will grow and change. It will become a butterfly.

The lessons in this chapter help you understand how living things, including yourself, change as they grow.

1 Observing How People Change

2 How Are Animals Born?

3 What Are Some Animal Life Cycles?

# 1 Observing How People Change

All animals grow and change. The caterpillar in the picture will become a butterfly. A mealworm will become a beetle. Tadpoles grow into frogs. But not all young animals change as much as caterpillars, mealworms, and tadpoles. Puppies and kittens change a little. But they look much like dogs and cats.

You were once a baby like the ones in the pictures. You have changed a lot since then! You will change more as you grow older. Look at the baby pictures of your classmates. Try to match each pupil to a picture. Notice how your classmates have changed. List three ways children change as they grow. Discuss your list with your classmates. How are the lists alike? How are they different?

## Think About It

1. How is the way people change different from the way caterpillars change?
2. **Challenge** What do you think the babies in the pictures will look like when they are your age?

These babies will change as they grow older

# 2 How Are Animals Born?

This baby chick is breaking its egg shell with its beak. A chick must peck for more than an hour to break out of the shell. When it gets out of the egg, the chick is tired and its feathers are wet. It rests as its feathers dry. Soon it can run around and find food.

Many kinds of animals lay eggs. Some, such as fish and frogs, lay eggs in the water. Others, such as birds and turtles, lay eggs on land. The shell keeps these land eggs from drying out.

Before it hatches, the young animal lives on food stored in the egg. The egg of a starfish is about the size of this dot. • The growing starfish uses up all the food in its egg in just a few days. A frog's egg has enough food for a growing frog for more than a week. An ostrich grows in its egg using food that lasts about forty days.

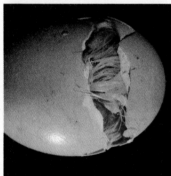

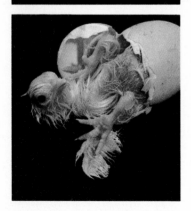

A chick works hard to get out of its shell

These young garter snakes hatched inside their mother's body

Many animals do not protect their eggs or young. Fish and insects lay hundreds or thousands of eggs at a time. Many eggs and young animals die or are eaten by other animals. But some stay alive. Some grow to become adults and have young—or **reproduce.** Fish and insects must lay many eggs so that at least *some* young will survive.

reproduce (rē′prə düs′), produce offspring.

Other animals protect their eggs and care for the young. A female wolf spider spins a sac around her eggs. She carries the egg sac with her. Young spiders cling to their mother's body for a week or more after hatching.

Most birds have only a few eggs in the nest at one time. Some birds, such as chickens, can find their own food soon after they hatch. But most birds are helpless when they first hatch. Parent birds feed them. The parents care for the young birds and protect them. Animals that protect and care for their young have fewer young.

The eggs of a few animals, such as garter snakes, guppies, and some sharks, hatch inside the mother's body. The young garter snakes in the picture grew inside soft-shelled eggs in their mother's body. The young snakes hatched inside their mother's body and were born alive.

### Have You Heard?
The sturgeon (stėr′jən), a kind of fish, lays as many as 7 million eggs each year. A termite queen can lay 30 thousand eggs in a day.

## What Are Mammals?

The young of some animals, such as cats, dogs, cows, and horses, are well developed when they are born. A calf grows inside its mother's body. As it grows, it gets food from its mother's body. After the calf is born, the cow cares for it. The young calf feeds on its mother's milk, like the calf in the picture. An animal that feeds on its mother's milk is a **mammal.** Some mammals, such as colts and calves, can run soon after they are born. Other baby mammals, such as the ape in the picture, are helpless for a long time. The animals on this page are mammals. You are a mammal too.

**mammal** (mam′əl), animal whose young feeds on milk produced by the mother.

A monkey parent cares for its young

### Think About It

1. How do mammals develop and care for their young differently from other animals?
2. What is the function of the shell of an egg?
3. **Challenge** What might happen if a bird laid hundreds of eggs at a time?

A calf feeding on its mother's milk

# Do You Know?

## What Are Wombats and Wallabies?

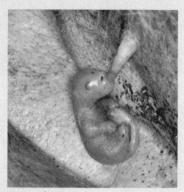
Young kangaroo

Wombat

Have you ever seen a wombat? Do you know what a wallaby looks like? These names may sound like they come from a book by Dr. Seuss. But both of these creatures are real animals. They belong to a group of mammals known as marsupials (mär sü′pē əlz).

Only one kind of marsupial—the opossum—lives in North America. Most marsupials live in Australia.

These animals are different from other mammals. The female marsupial has a pouch.

A kangaroo is a marsupial. The picture shows a baby kangaroo inside its mother's pouch. Notice how small the baby is. A newborn kangaroo is about the size of a honeybee!

When a marsupial is born, it crawls over the mother's body, looking for her pouch. Once inside the pouch, the baby attaches itself to the mother's nipple, as shown, and drinks her milk. The baby stays attached to the nipple, in the pouch for weeks or months. Later, the young animal leaves the pouch for short periods of time. But suppose danger approaches or it begins to rain. The young marsupial scampers back to the safety and warmth of its mother's pouch. Some young marsupials dive headfirst into the pouch when they are frightened.

Besides the kangaroo, many other marsupials live in Australia, New Zealand, and the nearby islands. Wallabies and whiptails are similar to kangaroos. A wombat, shown here, looks like a woodchuck and digs holes in the ground.

Koala

The koala is a marsupial that spends its life in trees. This animal eats the leaves from only one kind of tree. By looking at the picture, you can see why the koala is called the teddy bear of Australia.

# 3 What Are Some Animal Life Cycles?

**life cycle** (sī′kəl), stages in the life of a living thing from birth to death.

**metamorphosis** (met′ə môr′fə sis), a complete change in form of an animal during its life cycle. [Plural: metamorphoses (met′ə môr′fə sēz′).]

You began as a baby. Now, you are a child. You will grow and change as you get older. You will continue to change even when you are an adult. The older people in the picture look different from the younger ones.

Animals, too, change as they grow older. All the stages from birth to death make up the **life cycle.** Young animals are born, grow and change, and become adults. The adults reproduce, and the new young repeat the life cycle. Growing older is part of the life cycle. Death is also a part of the life cycle. Some animals do not live to reach old age. They die of illness or are eaten by other animals.

Some animals change slowly. Others change quickly and completely. A complete change in form is called **metamorphosis.**

Older people look different from younger people

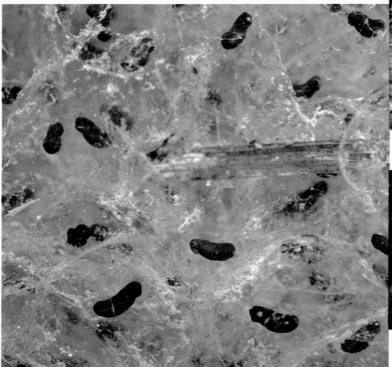

Eggs

Tadpole

Older tadpole

Frog

## What Are the Stages in the Life Cycle of a Frog?

The pictures show the stages in the life cycle of a frog. A female frog lays several thousand eggs in the water. The eggs hatch into tadpoles that do not look like frogs at all. They look like little black or brown fish. They have big heads and long tails. They have gills and live under water. As a tadpole grows, its tail becomes smaller. Find the legs forming on the growing tadpole. Lungs are growing inside the tadpole. When the lungs are large enough, the animal can breathe out of the water. The tadpole is now a young frog. The change from tadpole to adult frog is a metamorphosis.

The frog climbs out of the water. Now it can live on land or in water. It can swim with its webbed feet. The female frog will lay eggs. The life cycle will begin again and repeat itself over and over.

### Have You Heard?

The male Darwin's frog of South America protects its young. It carries the eggs and tadpoles in its mouth. When the tadpoles change into frogs, they jump out of the parent's mouth.

25

## What Are the Stages in the Life Cycle of a Butterfly?

The pictures show the stages in a butterfly's life cycle. Butterflies lay eggs on trees or plants. The egg is the first stage in a butterfly's life cycle. Caterpillars hatch from the eggs. Only one or two of every hundred caterpillars live to become adults. A caterpillar is the second stage—or **larva**—of the butterfly. A larva is a young animal that looks very different from the adult.

A caterpillar eats all the time. It eats once or twice its weight in leaves every day. A caterpillar grows rapidly. Its skin does not grow as fast as the caterpillar grows. When the skin becomes too tight, it splits. The caterpillar crawls out of its old skin. A new, bigger skin grows.

A fully grown caterpillar attaches itself to a leaf or branch. Then, it begins the next stage of its metamorphosis. It changes into a **pupa.** A hard, shiny covering protects the pupa. Inside the hard case, the caterpillar's body changes into a butterfly. After a few weeks, the hard case around the pupa splits open. An adult butterfly comes out.

Some caterpillars spin a silky thread case—or **cocoon**—around themselves. A cocoon, like the one in the picture, protects the pupa. A moth comes out of the cocoon. Silk cloth is made from threads from the cocoons of certain caterpillars.

**larva** (lär′və), the young of an animal that is different in form from the adult. [Plural: larvae (lär′vē).]

**pupa** (pyü′pə), stage in the insect life cycle between larva and adult. [Plural: pupae (pyü′pē).]

**cocoon** (kə kün′), case of silky thread spun by some insect larvae in which the pupa lives.

Cocoon

### Find Out
Use library books to find out the difference between butterflies and moths.

Eggs and larvae

Adult

Pupa

Larva

27

Adult cicada climbs out of its old skin

**nymph** (nimf), stage in the life cycle of some insects between egg and adult that looks like the adult but has no wings.

## What Are the Stages in the Life Cycles of a Cockroach and a Cicada?

A few insects, such as cockroaches, grasshoppers, and crickets, have a different metamorphosis. The pictures show the stages of the life cycle of a cockroach. Cockroaches lay eggs in egg cases that protect them. The young cockroach—or **nymph**—looks almost like an adult. But it is smaller and has no wings. A nymph sheds its skin several times as it grows. An adult cockroach looks like its parents. An adult female lays eggs that hatch into new cockroach nymphs.

The life cycle of a cicada (sə kā′də) is like that of the cockroach. Cicadas lay eggs in trees. After an egg hatches, the nymph drops to the ground and digs into the soil. It gets new, bigger skin several times while under the ground. Then, it climbs up and onto a tree. The nymph's skin splits down the back and an adult climbs out. Notice in the picture how the old skin clings to the tree.

### Think About It

1. How is a nymph different from a larva?
2. Describe the stages in the life cycle of the human, frog, butterfly, and cockroach.
3. **Challenge** Do mammals and birds go through metamorphosis? Explain your answer.

Find Out!
Use the library to find out why the periodical cicada is sometimes called the seventeen-year locust.

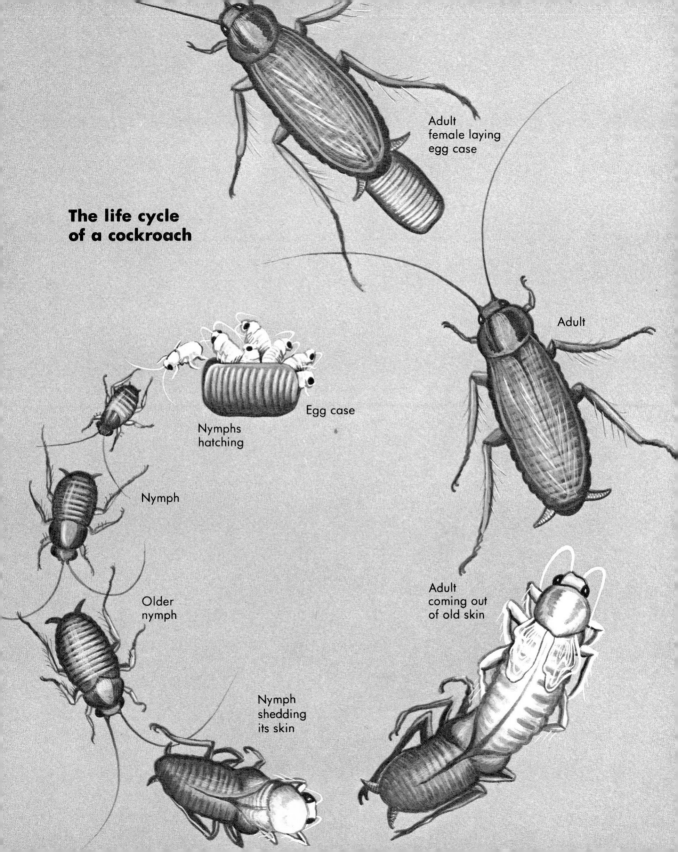

**The life cycle of a cockroach**

Adult female laying egg case

Adult

Nymphs hatching

Egg case

Nymph

Older nymph

Adult coming out of old skin

Nymph shedding its skin

# Activity

## Observing Stages in the Life Cycle of Mealworms

**Purpose**
To identify the different stages in the life cycle of mealworms.

**You Will Need**
- small glass jar with holes punched in its lid
- handful of bran or cereal flakes
- mealworms
- paper towel
- piece of potato, apple, or other moist food
- hand lens

**Directions**
1. Put some cereal in the bottom of your jar. Add a few mealworms to the jar.
2. Place a piece of paper towel on top of the cereal. Place a piece of moist food on the paper towel.

3. Record what your mealworms look like. What color are they? Measure how long they are. Look at a mealworm closely with a hand lens. How many eyes, legs, and body segments does it have?
4. Put the jar in a warm place out of direct sunlight or direct heat.
5. Observe your mealworms at least once a week. Clean out old pieces of moist food and put in fresh pieces.
6. Record any changes in the mealworms' size or what they look like. The mealworms are larvae. Look for pupae and beetles, like the ones in the pictures.

**Think About It**

1. Draw the stages you saw in the life cycle of the mealworm. Label the stages in your drawing.
2. **Challenge** How is the life cycle of a mealworm like the life cycle of a caterpillar? How is it different?

Beetle

Pupa

# Tie It Together

## Sum It Up

1. How is the way mammals develop different from the way birds and fish develop? Explain in a few sentences.

2. Each lettered drawing shows a stage in the life cycle of an animal. On a sheet of paper, show the stages in the life cycles of a frog, a butterfly, and a cockroach. In the life cycles, use the letters of the drawings below and draw the missing stages.

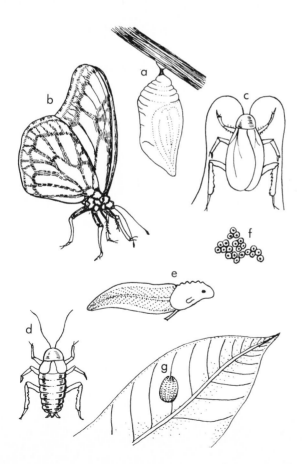

## Challenge!

1. What might happen to plants that caterpillars eat if all the eggs that butterflies laid survived to become caterpillars?

2. How are a frog's eggs different from a bird's eggs?

3. What might happen to a newborn baby mammal if its mother died?

4. A tadpole is a stage of a frog's life cycle. What stage of a butterfly's life cycle is it most like?

5. What stage of a butterfly's metamorphosis is missing in a cockroach's life cycle?

## Science Words

cocoon

larva

life cycle

mammal

metamorphosis

nymph

pupa

reproduce

# Laboratory

## Responding to a Stimulus

*a*

### Purpose
To observe how organisms respond to changes in temperature.

### You Will Need
- paper punch
- 3 plastic margarine tubs
- marking pen
- 2 pans
- plastic straws
- centimeter ruler
- glue
- soil
- ant food
- ants
- clear-plastic food wrap
- masking tape
- hot tap water
- ice-cold water
- 2 thermometers

### Stating the Problem
All organisms respond to changes in their environments. Can you predict how ants would respond to temperature changes? Do you think ants would move away from food if the

*b*

*c*

temperature near the food became too hot or too cold? Record your prediction and the reasons for it.

### Investigating the Problem
1. Punch 2 holes on opposite sides of a margarine tub about halfway from the top, as shown in picture *a*. Punch a single hole the same distance from the top in the other 2 tubs.
2. Label one of the pans *hot* and the other *cold*. Place a margarine tub with a single hole into each of the pans. Place the 3 tubs in a row, as shown in picture *b*.
3. Connect the 3 tubs by inserting plastic straws through the holes, as shown in picture *c*. Let the ends of the straws

reach about 2 cm into the tubs. Use glue to seal any open spaces between the tubs and the inserted straws. Let the glue dry.

4. Fill the 3 tubs with soil to the level of the straws, as shown in picture *d*.

5. Place sweet-tasting food, such as sugar or cake crumbs, into the 2 end tubs.

6. Place the ants in the middle tub. Cover each tub with clear-plastic wrap. Tape the 2 end margarine tubs to the large pans as shown in picture *e*. Observe the movement of the ants for about 15 minutes.

7. Pour hot tap water into the pan labeled *hot* and ice-cold water into the other pan. Record the water temperatures. *CAUTION: The mercury in a thermometer is poisonous. Do not touch*

e

the mercury if a thermometer breaks.

8. Observe the movement of the ants for about 15 minutes. Record all your observations. After 15 minutes, record the temperature of the water in the pans.

**Making Conclusions**

1. Did the ants respond to the food before the tubs were placed in hot and cold water? If so, how did the ants respond?

2. Did the ants respond to the hot and cold temperatures? If so, how?

3. What change in the environment had to occur for the ants to return to the food tubs?

4. Was your prediction about the ants' response to temperature change correct? Explain.

d

# Careers

## Kennel Owner

"I guess the main reason I opened a kennel," says Sue, "is because this area needed one. About five years ago I was raising German shepherds. Back then, I had a hard time finding a boarding kennel. So, I thought I might as well open my own."

People bring their pets to stay at Sue's kennel. The pets stay for a few hours to a few months.

"Many of our customers are people who are moving or going on vacation. They bring their pets here, and we take care of them. Most of the animals are dogs and cats, but we have also taken care of rabbits, birds, and guinea pigs."

Sue's working day begins about 7:30 in the morning, when the animals are fed. "At 8:00 people start arriving to check their pets in and out. We are usually busy until 8:00 or 10:00 at night.

"The dogs have indoor and outdoor runs. They get plenty of exercise. I also have a person who grooms all the animals.

"The best part of this job is working with animals and seeing all the different breeds of dogs. It is also interesting to work with the different personalities of the pets."

Sue says that some of the animals can get homesick. "A dog might miss its owner and take a while to get used to the new surroundings. For one or two days the dog may eat very little and just lie in the corner. We might give the dog a treat or some fresh meat. Then, the dog usually begins eating more and will be all right. If we think the animal is really ill, we take it right to the vet."

Sue hires many people to help her care for the animals. "I expect the workers to like animals and to not have any fear of handling them. I also expect them either to be going to school or to have a high-school education."

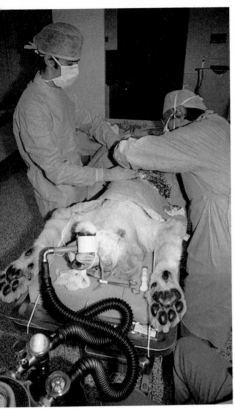

Veterinarian

One of the easiest ways to see how animals live is to go to a zoo. Besides seeing animals, you can see the results of many hardworking people.

Most zoos begin with a **zoo designer**—or zoo planner. This person must study the natural surroundings of the animals that will live in the zoo. The designer tries to provide a setting for each animal that will match these surroundings. Designers must also know about an animal's habits. Some animals jump or burrow. Some sleep in a den or swim in a pool. Designers must be aware of these needs in order to keep the animals happy and healthy.

Once the animals are at the zoo, the **veterinarian** helps keep them healthy. Each day, the veterinarian checks on any sick or injured animals. Veterinarians may operate on some animals.

The veterinarian works closely with the **nutritionist.** It is the nutritionist's job to plan the animals' meals and to order the large amounts of food.

**Zoo keepers** often become the most trusted friends of the animals. The keepers work closely with the animals every day. They clean the cages, feed the animals, and keep daily records of the animals' behaviors.

Some zoo keepers are also animal trainers. They teach the animals how to move on command so that cages can be cleaned. A trained animal is also easier to feed and to inspect for illness.

Many people like animals and enjoy being around them. But many jobs in a zoo require more than just a fondness for animals. Students who want to become designers, veterinarians, or nutritionists graduate from college and attend classes after college. Students who graduate from high school can become trainers and keepers.

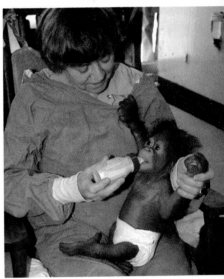

Zoo keeper

# On Your Own

## Picture Clue

Look at the picture on page 2. Can you tell what the object is? The picture on page 15 shows worker bees inside a bee hive. Compare the pictures to find out what the object on page 2 is.

## Projects

1. Look under rocks, logs, or beneath plants for snails and slugs. Design an experiment to find out what kind of food a snail or slug eats. What response does it have to light and other stimuli?

2. Some animals can take care of themselves just after they are born. The human baby is helpless and needs a lot of care. Use reference books in the library to find some advantages and disadvantages of needing a lot of care.

3. Grasshoppers spend the winter as eggs, cicadas as nymphs, cecropia moths as pupae, and frogs as adults. Observe some insects outside in the fall. In what stage will they spend the winter?

4. Dye some birdseed with food coloring. Use the dyed birdseed in an experiment to find out if birds prefer certain colors.

## Books About Science

*Animals That Live in Groups* by Jane E. Hartman. Holiday House, 1979. Learn how animals that live in societies behave.

*Grasshoppers* by Jane Dallinger. Lerner, 1981. Describes the life cycle of the grasshopper and explains how grasshoppers cause damage to crops.

*Spiders* by Sarah R. Riedman. Watts, 1979. Tells how different kinds of spiders behave and where they live.

*What's Hatching Out of That Egg?* by Patricia Lauber. Crown, 1979. Find out what kinds of animals hatch from a variety of eggs.

# Unit Test

## Multiple Choice

Number your paper from 1–5. Next to each number, write the letter of the word or words that best complete the statement or answer the question.

1. Mammals are different from other animals because they
   a. hatch from eggs.
   b. go through a life cycle.
   c. go through metamorphosis.
   d. feed on milk produced by the mother.

2. Animals that live in a society
   a. cannot communicate with each other.
   b. do jobs needed to keep the society going.
   c. live in hives.
   d. live on stored food in winter.

3. The three stages in the life cycle of a frog are the tadpole, adult, and
   a. egg.
   b. larva.
   c. nymph.
   d. pupa.

4. A spider knows how to spin a web
   a. because an adult spider taught it.
   b. because it lives in a society.
   c. by instinct.
   d. when it becomes an adult.

5. When animals have a complete change of form during their life cycle, the change is called
   a. reproduction.
   b. metamorphosis.
   c. stimulus.
   d. communication.

## Matching

Number your paper from 6–10. Read the description in Column I. Next to each number, write the letter of the word or words from Column II that best match the description in Column I.

**Column I**

6. give or receive information that is understood

7. an activity that occurs because of a stimulus

8. the way a living thing acts

9. stage of life of a butterfly in which it spends all its time eating

10. young insect that looks almost like the adult

**Column II**

a. nymph

b. communicate

c. behavior

d. response

e. larva

# UNIT TWO
# WEATHER

Like the water
   and the sky
Having a disagreement.
Crashing together
   with a burst
   of feeling.

Joyce Shin *age 10*

# Chapter 3

# Elements of Weather

The flight of the colorful hot-air balloons depends upon the weather. A balloonist carefully checks temperature, wind, and cloud conditions before taking off into the sky.

Weather is important to everybody. Will it be warm enough to go swimming? Will crops get the rain they need? Will it be too windy to ride a bicycle? The answers to questions like these affect our lives every day.

The lessons in this chapter will help you understand the weather, including temperature, wind, clouds, and rain.

1 Measuring the Sun's Effect on Temperature

2 What Causes Different Temperatures?

3 How Does Air Move?

4 How Does Water Get into the Air?

5 How Do We Get Rain?

# 1 Measuring the Sun's Effect on Temperature

The boy in the picture was working in the hot sunlight all day. But now he rests in the cool shade of a tree where much of the sunlight cannot reach him. The air temperature of a place depends greatly on how much sunlight reaches the place.

You can find out how sunlight affects air temperature. Place a thermometer in a shady spot. After five minutes, record the temperature. Move the thermometer to a sunny spot. Wait five minutes, and record the temperature again.

## Think About It

1. What was the difference in degrees between the temperatures in the sun and in the shade?
2. **Challenge** Why is the daytime usually warmer than the nighttime?

# 2 What Causes Different Temperatures?

A sunny day does not always mean a warm day. In fact, in the northern United States, some of the coldest winter days are sunny.

The amount of sunlight reaching a certain place causes different temperatures. In summer the sun rises early and sets late. We have more hours of daylight. In winter the sun rises late and sets early. We have fewer hours of daylight.

The round shape of our planet helps cause different temperatures around the world. In the drawing, notice how sunlight shines directly on *A*—near the equator. But as you move away from the equator, toward *B*, sunlight shines on the earth at an angle because the earth's surface curves. The total amount of sunlight is the same at *A* as it is at *B*. But sunlight is spread out over more of the earth's surface at *B*. Sunlight is packed into a smaller space at *A*. So the air temperature near *A* is higher than near *B*.

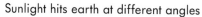

Sunlight hits earth at different angles

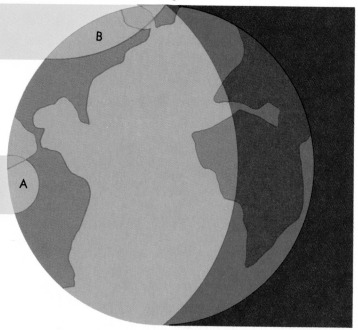

Cool and warm grass

Water also affects temperature. The temperature of the air near an ocean or large lake is often different from the temperature away from the water. Water warms up more slowly than land. On a hot day at the beach, the water is cooler than the sand. The cool water cools the air nearby. People living near an ocean are often cooler than those far from the water.

But on a cold day the water may be warmer than the sandy beach. Water cools off much more slowly than land. In winter, people living near the ocean are often warmer than those away from the water.

The type of land surface can affect the temperature of that surface. If you walk barefoot over a blacktop driveway on a hot, sunny day, you might jump off quickly. Dark objects, such as the driveway, absorb—or take in—more of the sun's heat than light-colored objects do.

The water, driveway, and sunny and shady grass shown here all absorb different amounts of heat. They all have different temperatures.

## Think About It

1. How do the hours of daylight affect temperature?
2. List three things that can affect temperature.
3. **Challenge** Why might it be a good idea to wear light-colored clothing in summer?

Hot driveway

Cool water

# 3 How Does Air Move?

air pressure (presh′ər), weight of the air.

## Find Out

Use an atlas to find out which city normally has higher air pressure, Denver or New York? Why?

The glider pilot in the picture is enjoying a wonderful view of the earth. Even though the glider has no engine, the pilot knows that moving air will give him a long, pleasant ride.

Air is made of gases you cannot see. Yet air has weight that presses down on the earth. The weight of air is called **air pressure.** Right now, about 1,000 kilograms of air, which is about the mass of a small car, is pressing against your whole body. But air pressure does not crush us. Air pressure inside our bodies presses outward as much as the outside air presses inward. Therefore, we do not feel the air pressing against us.

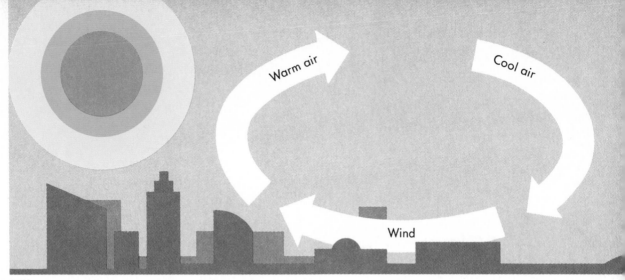

Differences in air pressure cause wind

The higher you are above the earth's surface, the lower the air pressure. Air pressure drops as you move up a mountain. The weight of the air pressing down is less as you go higher into the sky. Some airplanes fly where the air pressure is very low. People are not able to breathe where air pressure is very low. Air pressure inside the airplane must be kept high enough for people to breathe comfortably.

Air pressure changes when sunlight heats some parts of the earth more than other parts. When the outside air in a certain place is heated, it becomes lighter and pushes down with less pressure. An area of lower pressure forms. The drawing shows how cooler air with higher pressure moves in to take the place of the warm air. Air moves from places of higher pressure to places of lower pressure. This moving air is wind.

When you blow air into a balloon, air pressure changes the balloon's shape. Air from your breath presses against the insides of the balloon. It becomes round and firm. As the air is let out, you can feel the "wind." It moves from a place of high pressure to a place of lower pressure.

### Have You Heard?

When people move from the coastal areas to the high Rocky Mountains, they often feel sluggish and tired much of the time. Their bodies have to get used to the lower air pressure and less amount of oxygen.

## How Do We Measure Wind?

The football kicker tosses blades of grass into the air to see how they fall. The kicker then knows how the wind will blow the ball. But the odd-looking instruments in the picture give us better ways of measuring wind direction and wind speed.

The **wind vane** measures wind direction. Wind hits the large tail and moves the vane until the arrow points into the wind. If the arrow points north, the wind is coming from that direction. It is called a north wind.

The **anemometer** measures wind speed. Wind hits the cups and turns them. The stronger the wind, the faster the cups turn. The turning cups are connected to a dial which shows the wind speed.

**wind vane** (vān), instrument that measures wind direction.

**anemometer** (an′ə mom′ə tər), instrument that measures wind speed.

## Think About It

1. What is wind?
2. What does an anemometer measure?
3. **Challenge** When you let the air out of a balloon, when does the "wind" stop coming out?

Football player tests the wind

Wind vane

Anemometer

# Do You Know?

## What Is the Wind Capital?

Chicago has long been called the Windy City. Many people who walk downtown might agree with this name. But the winds in Chicago are really not that strong. They only average 16 kilometers per hour.

Boston is one of the windiest cities in the United States. The average wind speed is 20 kilometers per hour. But it is Mount Washington, New Hampshire, that stands out as the wind capital of the United States—and of the world.

The average wind speed on Mount Washington is about 56 kilometers per hour—the greatest in the United States. The strongest of these winds was recorded on April 12, 1934. On that day the wind roared across the mountain's peak at 372 kilometers per hour! This wind speed is the strongest ever recorded in the world, except during tornadoes. On about 100 days every year, the wind on Mount Washington is as strong as it is in a hurricane!

Besides strong winds, Mount Washington has heavy snowfalls and bitter-cold temperatures.

For over fifty years this weather information has been observed and recorded by people who work at the Mount Washington Observatory. To get this information, these people experience one of the harshest combinations of wind, cold, and ice in the world.

Wind adds to harsh weather

# 4 How Does Water Get into the Air?

**evaporate** (i vap/ə rāt/), change from a liquid into a gas.

**water vapor** (vā/pər), water that is in the form of gas.

**condense** (kən dens/), change from a gas into a liquid.

## Have You Heard?

In the deserts, people have learned to put every drop of water to use. One custom is to dig a pit around a fruit tree and to line the pit with stones. At night the stones cool off quickly, and drops of moisture condense on the stones. The water trickles down to the roots of the tree to keep it alive.

During a rainstorm you can easily see water in the air. But some water is *always* in the air—even in a desert.

If you toss a bucketful of water into the air, it does not suddenly disappear. The water may fall on a sidewalk and make a large wet mark. Soon the wet mark gets smaller and smaller until the sidewalk is dry. What happens to the water?

Heat causes the water to slowly **evaporate**—or change from a liquid into an invisible gas. The gas is **water vapor.** Water evaporates into the air from oceans, lakes, rivers, and even from your body.

When water vapor cools, it may **condense**—or change back into a liquid. Water vapor is in the boy's warm breath. The vapor cools and condenses as it meets the cold air. He can see his breath.

Water vapor in breath condenses

Fog rolling over San Francisco Bay

Have You Heard?

The drops of water that form clouds are so small that 50 billion drops would not even fill a cup.

Air with much water vapor

## How Do Clouds Form?

The condensed water vapor from the boy's breath is really a small cloud. The larger clouds in the sky form in much the same way.

As air warms, it becomes lighter and rises. But as the warm air rises higher, it cools. Water vapor in the air condenses. Tiny drops of water form. Together, all these tiny drops of water form clouds.

Sometimes air does not rise on its own. Instead, it is forced upward. When air bumps into a mountain, some of the air is forced upward, as shown. The air cools, and water vapor condenses to form clouds over the mountain.

Sometimes air near the ground is cooled. If this air has a lot of water vapor, the vapor condenses. A cloud near the ground—or fog—forms. You often see fog when warm, moist air moves over cold ground or water. The cold surface cools the air. This cooling causes the water vapor to condense, and fog forms. The picture shows how thick fog can get. When you walk in a fog, you are walking in a cloud. You feel the wetness around you. But you cannot feel each drop of moisture because it is too small.

49

Cumulus

Stratus

Cirrus

## What Kinds of Clouds Are There?

Many people enjoy gazing at clouds. Winds often blow them into shapes of animals and people. You often see clouds like those in the pictures.

**Cirrus** clouds are thin and feathery looking. They float very high in the air and are made of tiny pieces of ice.

Notice how **stratus** clouds spread in sheets across the sky. These low clouds may cover the whole sky. Stratus clouds often bring rain.

You can see that **cumulus** clouds look like pieces of cotton. Cumulus clouds are usually a sign of fair weather. But at other times a cumulus cloud develops into a thunderhead and brings rain.

**cirrus** (sir′əs), high feathery-looking clouds made of tiny pieces of ice.

**stratus** (strat′əs), clouds in sheets or layers that spread over a large area.

**cumulus** (kyü′myə ləs), clouds that look like piles of cotton.

### Think About It

1. What happens to water vapor when it condenses?
2. How does a cloud form?
3. **Challenge** Do cirrus clouds form where the air is warm or cold? Explain your answer.

# Activity

## Comparing Different Speeds of Evaporation

### Purpose
To compare how water evaporates in warm air and in cold air.

### You Will Need
- 2 jars of equal size
- covers for the jars
- 2 pieces of cloth, about 3 cm on each side
- needle
- thread (10 cm)
- tape
- water

### Directions
1. Put one jar in sunlight or near a heating vent for about 30 minutes. Put the other jar in a refrigerator for the same time. Do not cover the jars.
2. Use the needle to bring the thread through one piece of cloth, as shown. Tie the thread to the cloth. Do the same for the other piece of cloth.
3. Tape a piece of thread to the inside of each jar cover, as the picture shows.
4. Wet each cloth, and gently squeeze out any extra water.
5. Remove the jars from the warm and cold places. Put the covers on the jars so that each cloth hangs into a jar, as shown in the picture.
6. Put the jars back in the warm and cold places for 30 more minutes.
7. Remove the jars and covers, and feel the cloths.

### Think About It
1. Which cloth is drier?
2. Where did the water from the cloths go?
3. Which held more water vapor, the warm air or the cold air?
4. **Challenge** How would leaving both jars in the same place change the results of this activity?

# 5 How Do We Get Rain?

When you take a hot shower, a patch of moisture may appear on a mirror. Vapor from the hot water condenses on the cool mirror. The condensed water drops are small and light enough to stay on the mirror. The picture shows what happens if you run your finger through the moisture. Your finger pushes the drops together to make larger drops. The large drops are heavy enough to run down the mirror.

Raindrops form almost the same way. Clouds are made of tiny drops of water. These drops are so light they float in the air. Drops can bump into each other and form larger, heavier drops. When the drops get large enough, they can no longer float in the air. Then, they fall as rain.

The drawing compares the size of a raindrop with the size of a drop that is part of a cloud. The drawing makes the drops look larger than they truly are. One cloud drop is really too small to see.

**Precipitation** is moisture that falls to the ground. Rain is just one form of precipitation. Moisture also falls as sleet, snow, and hail.

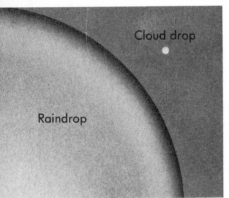

Cloud drop

Raindrop

Comparing drop sizes

During winter, rain may fall through a very cold layer of air. The rain freezes and forms into little pieces of ice called sleet.

Sometimes the rain does not freeze until it hits the cold ground or a cold object. Then, everything becomes coated with ice, as shown.

The air high above the ground is cold. So, if a cloud is high enough, it will be made of tiny bits of ice. The bits of ice are little snowflakes. The snowflakes join and begin to fall. In summer a layer of warm air changes the snowflakes into raindrops. But during the cold months of winter, snowflakes continue to fall as snow. If the snow is wet, the flakes easily stick together. You may have noticed that wet snow packs well.

Hail or hailstones are balls of ice. Notice that a hailstone has many layers. Strong winds in cumulus clouds lift falling raindrops up into colder air. The raindrops become ice, fall, and are lifted again. Drops of water freeze around the pieces of ice as the ice moves up and down inside the clouds. When the hailstones become heavy enough, they fall to the ground.

**precipitation**
(pri sip′ə tā′shən), moisture that falls to the ground.

Layers of large hailstone

Wires and trees coated with ice

53

# How Do We Measure Precipitation?

## Have You Heard?

After a storm you may hear that 3 cm of rain fell. But the ground will not be covered with this much water because the ground is not completely flat. Rainwater moves downhill into rivers, ditches, and sewers. Also, much rainwater soaks into the soil, and some evaporates.

Weather reporters tell you how much rain and snow falls to the ground. You could measure the rainfall just by setting a pan outside. But very small amounts of rainfall are hard to measure this way.

Rainfall is best measured with a **rain gauge.** The rain gauge in the picture is a funnel leading into a tube. Rainwater drops through the funnel and into the tube. The tube is marked so a person can easily read the water level.

Snowfall is measured by simply pushing a ruler into the snow. You can read the snow level on the ruler. When measuring snowfall, you should take readings in many places. You should not measure the snow where wind has blown it into a snowdrift.

## Think About It

1. How does a raindrop form?
2. List four kinds of precipitation.
3. **Challenge** How can hail form on a warm day?

Weather observer using rain gauge

# Tie It Together

## Sum It Up

On a sheet of paper, unscramble the words in capital letters to complete the sentences.

1. The amount of *LISGUNHT* reaching an area affects the temperature.

2. One reason the earth's surface has different temperatures is that sunlight shines *IRTLECDY* on some parts of the earth but at an *GLNEA* on other parts.

3. *RIA SRERPEUS* gets less as you rise higher above the earth.

4. Air moving is called *NDWI*.

5. An *MERANTOEME* measures wind speed.

6. All air holds some *RWAET PVARO*.

7. Water vapor *DCOENESNS* to form *DOULCS*.

8. Rain, snow, sleet, and hail are different kinds of *NPECTOIPRIITA*.

## Challenge!

1. On a hot, sunny day, would you probably be cooler in a white shirt or in a dark blue shirt? Explain your answer.

2. Explain how riding in an elevator in a skyscraper is an example of changing air pressure.

3. If you leave a glass of cold water outside on a hot day, beads of water will form on the outside of the glass. Explain where this water comes from and how it formed on the glass.

4. How can sleet and hail, which are both frozen water, look so different?

## Science Words

air pressure

anemometer

cirrus

condense

cumulus

evaporate

precipitation

rain gauge

stratus

water vapor

wind vane

# Chapter 4

# Air Masses and Storms

The day began bright and sunny. But rain had been forecast for the small Midwestern town later in the day. About noon, clouds began forming over distant fields. Soon, the faint rumble of thunder could be heard. People eating lunch outside headed for shelter as clouds blocked out the sun. A strange green glow suddenly gave the area a scary appearance. Townspeople shook with fear when they saw the funnel-shaped cloud dangling in the sky. The funnel touched the ground, destroying everything in its path. Cars were lifted like plastic toys and tossed through the air. Brick and wooden buildings blew apart. The deadly tornado had struck!

The lessons in this chapter will help you learn about storms and how to protect yourself when a storm strikes.

1 Observing the Mixture of Cold and Warm Water

2 What Are Air Masses and Fronts?

3 What Happens in a Thunderstorm?

4 What Are Hurricanes and Tornadoes?

5 How Are Weather Predictions Made?

# 1 Observing the Mixture of Cold and Warm Water

The picture below was taken from high above the earth. The line of clouds shows the border between two huge blocks of air. One block of air may be warm. Another block of air next to it may be cooler. You can do an activity to see what happens when warm and cool air meet.

Water and air often act in similar ways. In this activity you can use hot water to stand for warm air and cold water to stand for cooler air. Fill a large jar about two-thirds full with cold water. Then, fill a small jar with hot water. Stir three drops of food coloring into the hot water. Be sure the jar is filled to the rim. Now, place a small sheet of foil over the top of the small jar. Use a rubber band to hold the foil. Place the small jar on the bottom of the large jar of cold water, as shown. Use a pencil to poke a large hole in the foil. Observe and record what happens to the warm, colored water.

Poke pencil through foil

## Think About It

1. Where did the hot water go when you poked a hole in the foil?
2. **Challenge** What do you think happens when cool air meets warm air?

Clouds moving over land

# 2 What Are Air Masses and Fronts?

**air mass,** large block of air with similar temperature and moisture throughout.

**front,** place where 2 different air masses meet.

Think of a warm, sunny day in the park. Suddenly, the wind gets stronger. You feel chilly. Clouds appear out of nowhere. As you listen to the faint sounds of thunder, you know you may spend the rest of the day inside.

The weather often changes in minutes. These changes may take place as a large block of air—an **air mass**—moves over the earth's surface. An air mass is a giant body of air that has similar temperature and moisture throughout. Air masses are so large that just two or three can cover the whole United States.

The mass forms when air moves very slowly over one place on the earth's surface. The temperature and amount of moisture in an air mass depends on where it forms. An air mass that forms over a warm ocean will be mild and moist. An air mass that forms over cold land will be cold and dry. The map describes four kinds of air masses. The arrows show that air masses generally move from west to east across the United States.

The place where two air masses meet is called a **front.** When a front moves into your area, you can expect a change in the weather.

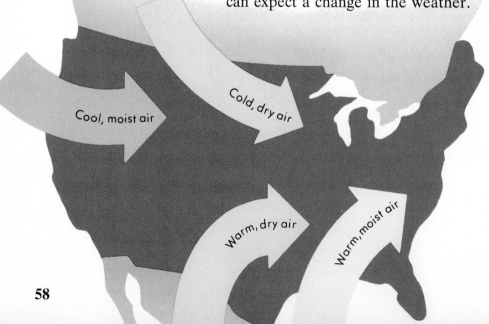

Cool, moist air

Cold, dry air

Warm, dry air

Warm, moist air

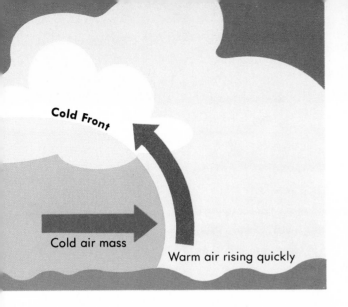

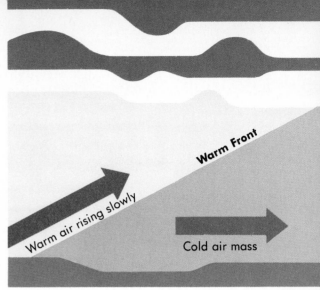

You may have heard the weather reporter speak of cold and warm fronts. A **cold front** is the boundary between a cold air mass and a warm air mass. A cold front forms when moving cold air bumps into warm air that is moving more slowly. The drawing of the cold front shows how cold air pushes under warm air. The warm air rises sharply, forming large, cumulus rain clouds. Thunderstorms or snowstorms are common at a cold front.

A **warm front** is the boundary between a warm air mass and a cold air mass. A warm front forms when moving warm air bumps into cold air that is moving more slowly. The drawing of the warm front shows how warm air glides up and over the cold air. Layers of stratus clouds form at a warm front. Steady rain or snow usually falls.

**cold front,** the boundary of a cold air mass moving into a slower-moving warm air mass.

**warm front,** the boundary of a warm air mass moving into a slower-moving cold air mass.

## Think About It

1. What is an air mass?
2. Describe the kinds of weather usually found at a cold front and at a warm front.
3. **Challenge** Describe an air mass that forms over the Pacific Ocean near the equator.

# 3 What Happens in a Thunderstorm?

You may have been awakened at night by the noise of a thunderstorm. Rain pours down upon the earth. Wind howls through the trees. After streaks of lightning dart across the sky, you can hear the roar of thunder.

Updrafts

Downdrafts

**updraft,** upward movement of air.

**downdraft,** downward movement of air.

## Have You Heard?

In 1956 updrafts kept a parachutist in the air for 40 minutes.

Thunderstorms usually happen in the spring and summer. A cold air mass pushes warm moist air upward. A cloud forms. The fast-rising air—or **updraft**—moves up through the cloud, as shown in the drawing. The cloud builds upward as air continues to rise and cool. Raindrops grow inside the cloud. When the raindrops fall, they drag air down through the cloud. This downward movement of air is a **downdraft.** Notice how a downdraft spreads out as it reaches near the ground. The downdrafts cause cool gusts of wind that tell us a thunderstorm is coming.

Lightning and thunder are part of a thunderstorm. Lightning flashes through the sky when electricity jumps from one cloud to another or between a cloud and the ground.

Rain

Notice that lightning looks like a single streak zigzagging across the sky. When lightning flashes between two clouds, you cannot always see the streak. It may be blocked out by the storm. But you can see how the streak makes the clouds glow.

A streak of lightning heats a narrow path of air to about 28,000° Celsius. This sudden heating of air causes the loud sound of thunder. If lightning is near you, the thunder sounds like a sharp crack. If the lightning is far away, the thunder sounds like a rumble.

You might experience something like lightning and thunder in your home. On a dry day you may get a shock from touching a piece of metal. If you listen, you can hear the crack. You may see a spark jump between the metal and your finger. The spark and crack are like lightning and thunder.

## How Can We Protect Ourselves from Lightning?

Lightning is very exciting to watch, but it can be very dangerous. Lightning causes fires and harms many people every year.

In the 1700s, Benjamin Franklin invented the **lightning rod** to help protect people from lightning. A lightning rod, shown in the drawing, is a metal rod placed on top of a building. Electricity travels rapidly through metal. The rod is connected to the ground by a cable. Lightning hits the rod and travels down the cable and into the ground. The electricity moves through the ground and does not harm the building. The picture shows a lightning rod at work on top of the Empire State Building in New York. Lightning rods are often used on farms to protect houses and barns.

Lightning rod protects house

**lightning rod,** metal rod on top of a building, used to carry lightning harmlessly to the ground.

Lightning rod at work on Empire State Building

Lightning split this tree

Lightning left its mark on these trees

The pictures tell you why you should not stand under a tree during a thunderstorm. Lightning usually strikes tall objects, such as towers, building tops, and trees. The power of a lightning bolt is shown on the trees above. Heat from the lightning can be so great that the tree explodes!

Open fields also are unsafe places to be during a thunderstorm. If you are standing in an open field, *you* may be the tallest object in the area. Lightning may be drawn toward you. If you must be outside, you should lie on the ground or in a low place, such as a ditch. If you are indoors, stay away from metal objects and wires. These objects can carry electricity. Lightning that hits a house travels rapidly along wires and through metal objects.

## Think About It

1. Explain how a thunderstorm forms.
2. What is lightning?
3. How does thunder form?
4. **Challenge** Why do you think tall buildings made with metal do not need lightning rods?

# 4 What Are Hurricanes and Tornadoes?

Every year about June, people in Florida begin to watch for bad weather. Powerful storms called hurricanes strike the Gulf and Atlantic coasts every summer. The storms move inland bringing clouds, strong winds, and heavy rain.

A hurricane is a strong, large, whirling group of clouds. Air pressure in a hurricane is very low. In the center of a hurricane is a calm region called the **eye.** Almost no rain falls in the eye. The sky may even be clear in the eye of a hurricane.

A hurricane begins over a tropical ocean. Warm, tropical water evaporates, and the water vapor condenses to form clouds and rain. As more and more water vapor condenses, the storm grows, and winds become stronger. When the winds reach 112 kilometers per hour, the storm is powerful enough to be called a hurricane. Warm water adds power to a hurricane as it moves across the ocean. But when the storm moves over land, warm water is no longer present. The storm dies out. The map shows the paths most hurricanes take in the United States.

**eye,** calm area in the center of a hurricane.

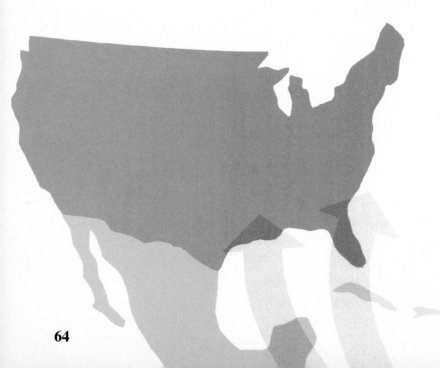

Wind and rain of hurricane

As the pictures show, hurricanes can do a great deal of damage when they reach land. Winds can reach 240 kilometers per hour. The wind from a hurricane flipped this airplane on its back. Heavy rains cause floods. These winds and floods often destroy buildings and kill thousands of people.

The people of the National Weather Service watch hurricanes closely. They try to tell where the storms will go and how strong they will be. Pictures taken from space show how hurricanes form and where they go. But to find out more about these storms, Air Force pilots fly right into hurricanes! The information the pilots gain will help us understand more about these deadly storms.

## How Do Tornadoes Form?

The most powerful winds on earth are in a tornado. Tornadoes cause less damage than hurricanes only because they are much smaller. Tornadoes form in violent thunderstorms where air is rising rapidly. If the air twists as it rises, it can become a funnel cloud—or a tornado. Winds in the funnel cloud reach 500 kilometers per hour.

Most tornadoes measure a few hundred meters across and last only a few minutes. But if the tornado touches the ground, it can destroy almost everything in its path. Notice the picture. You can find the path of a tornado by the destruction it left behind.

In the United States, tornadoes are most common in the South and Midwest. They usually occur from April to June. Many schools have tornado drills during this time.

### Think About It

1. Explain how a hurricane forms.
2. When and where do most tornadoes form?
3. **Challenge** Why do hurricanes hit Florida more than they hit New York?

# Do You Know?

## People Hunt Hurricanes

If you knew a hurricane was heading your way, you might want to know several other things. You would probably want to know exactly where the hurricane was going, how strong it was, and when it would hit your town. Hurricane hunters risk their lives to help answer these questions.

Hurricane hunters are Air Force pilots. Their job is to help study hurricanes by flying right into them!

As soon as a satellite picture shows that a hurricane is forming, the hurricane hunters go to work. They head for the storm in planes like the one in the picture. Notice the view they get once they reach the hurricane.

Weather scientists aboard the plane gather as much information as they can about the hurricane. They use instruments to measure the storm's air temperature, direction, speed, air pressure, and other elements of weather. Some of the instruments are dropped from the plane into the eye of the hurricane. The instruments send radio signals to the plane. The hurricane hunters radio the information to weather stations on land. Here, scientists use the information to make forecasts about the hurricane.

Hurricane hunters and the scientists on board the planes know their jobs can be dangerous. They must fly through winds that reach over 200 kilometers per hour. But they also know that flying into the hurricane is the best way to get useful information about these mighty storms.

Hurricane hunter's plane

View from inside hurricane

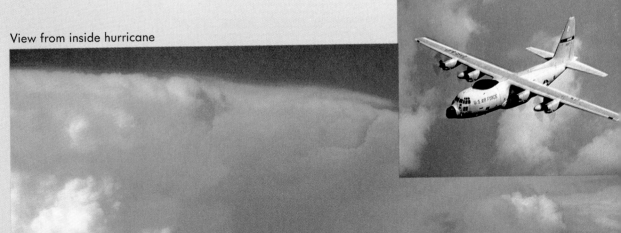

67

# 5 How Are Weather Predictions Made?

**meteorologist**
(mē′tē ə rol′ə jist), scientist who studies the weather.

**predict** (pri dikt′), tell about something before it happens.

**barometer** (bə rom′ə tər), instrument that measures air pressure.

You may wake up to a gray, rainy morning. But the weather report calls for clear skies by afternoon. How does a weather reporter know the weather will change so much in just a few hours?

**Meteorologists** are people who study the weather. They describe and try to **predict**—or forecast—the weather. To predict the weather, meteorologists study temperature, wind direction, air pressure, air masses, and other parts of weather.

A **barometer,** such as the one shown, measures air pressure. The needle moves as air pressure changes. Meteorologists also use wind vanes, thermometers, and other instruments every day.

We cannot get all the weather information we need from instruments on the ground. The weather balloon in the picture carries instruments high into the air. With the balloon we can learn about the weather as high as 40 kilometers above the earth. About 1,600 weather balloons are sent up all over the world every day.

Barometer

Weather balloon carries instruments

Satellite picture

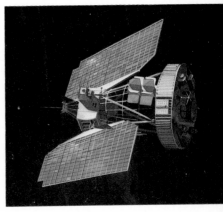

Weather satellite

Satellites, such as the one shown, circle the earth and help meteorologists predict the weather. The satellites carry cameras that take pictures of the earth. This satellite picture shows us where the clouds and storms are. By looking at several pictures, meteorologists can tell where clouds are moving and how the weather might change.

Meteorologists cannot always predict the weather correctly. As meteorologists learn more about what causes the weather, forecasting will improve.

## Think About It

1. Name three instruments meteorologists use to predict the weather.
2. How do satellites help predict weather?
3. **Challenge** If clear weather was to the west of you and a storm was to the east, what kind of weather might you predict for your area?

# Activity

## Making a Barometer

### Purpose
To measure and record air pressure.

### You Will Need
- balloon (already cut)
- baby-food jar
- rubber band
- glue
- toothpick
- paper straw
- sheet of cardboard
- small block of wood

### Directions
1. Stretch the cut balloon tightly over the mouth of the baby-food jar. Hold the balloon in place with the rubber band, as shown. Ask your teacher to check your work.
2. Flatten the paper straw.
3. Glue the toothpick to the straw to make a pointer, as shown.
4. Glue the straw to the center of the balloon. Hold the straw in place until it dries. You have made a barometer. The picture shows how it might look.

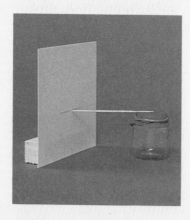

5. Glue the cardboard to the block of wood. Notice in the picture that the cardboard is straight.
6. Mark a line on the cardboard where the toothpick points.
7. Check the barometer each day for a week. On the cardboard, mark the new position of the pointer each day. Also, check the weather report each day to find out if air pressure is going up or going down. See if your barometer shows these changes in pressure.

### Think About It

1. What happened to the pointer when air pressure went up? Went down?
2. Did the weather change when the pointer moved?
3. **Challenge** How could your barometer help you predict the weather?

# Tie It Together

## Sum It Up

On a separate sheet of paper, complete each sentence begun in Column I by matching it to the correct ending in Column II. Write the complete sentence.

**Column I**

1. An air mass is a ▦
2. Warm air glides up over cold air at ▦
3. You can probably find thunderstorms at ▦
4. Air pressure in a hurricane is ▦
5. Meteorologists are ▦

**Column II**

a. a warm front.

b. very low.

c. a cold front.

d. people who study weather.

e. large block of air with similar temperature and moisture throughout.

## Challenge!

1. Describe an air mass that forms over northern Canada.

2. If a long pause comes between a lightning streak and its thunder, do you think the lightning is far away or close to you? Why?

3. Why do you think golfers sometimes get struck by lightning?

4. Name three kinds of storms that are caused by rising air.

## Science Words

air mass

barometer

cold front

downdraft

eye

front

lightning rod

meteorologist

predict

updraft

warm front

# Laboratory

## Making a Cloud

a

### Purpose
To infer how clouds form.

### You Will Need
- 2 aluminum pie plates
- crushed ice
- 2 large glass jars (liter size) with lids
- hot tap water
- ice-cold water

### Stating the Problem
The air is filled with invisible water vapor that forms clouds. What makes the water vapor in the air change into a cloud? Does warm air form clouds more easily than cold air? Make a cloud in a jar to learn how clouds form in the sky.

### Investigating the Problem

*Part I*
1. Place ice on one of the aluminum plates, as shown in picture *a*. Let the pie plates sit until you use them in step 3.

2. Fill 2 jars with very hot tap water. Cover the jars with the lids, and let them stand for 2 minutes.
3. Quickly empty the jars, and immediately cover them with the aluminum plates as shown in picture *b*.
4. Observe the insides of both jars. Record your observations.

*Part II*
1. Remove the aluminum plates from both jars. Leave the jars open for a short while.
2. Fill both jars with ice-cold water. Cover the jars, and let them stand for 2 minutes.
3. Empty the jars quickly. Immediately cover the

jars with the aluminum pie plates. One of the plates should have ice on it.
4. Observe the insides of both jars. Record your observations.

**Making Conclusions**
1. Was the temperature of the water in the jars important for the forming of clouds? How do you know?
2. What must have been present inside the jar to form a cloud? Where did it come from?
3. Was the ice needed to form a cloud? How do you know?
4. How did ice change the air in the jar in Part I?
5. From your observations of the different jars, describe the kind of air that forms clouds.
6. What must happen to this air before clouds can form?

b

# Careers

**Hurricane Hunter**

"I have always had a great respect for weather," says Sam, an Air Force major. "The power is awesome, and it can hit you in no time."

Sam joined the Air Force after high school, 14 years ago. While in the Air Force, he became interested in the weather. "To combine my interests in airplanes and weather, I started to work with the hurricane hunters."

"My job is really called weather reconnaissance (ri kon′ə səns). This means we use planes and satellites to collect weather information."

For the past eight years the Major has flown airplanes in and around hurricanes. "We enter a hurricane at about 3,200 meters. We enter the wall of clouds where the wind is the least dangerous. Then, we fly into the eye of the storm."

Part of the hurricane hunter's job is to find out exactly where the storm is located. Satellites are not always accurate enough for this purpose.

Hurricane hunters also measure the storm's size, wind speed, and air pressure. "But the most

important part of the job," says the Major, "is radioing the information back to the National Hurricane Center. After all, the information we collect does no good if we keep it to ourselves.

"Chemistry and physics courses in high school were helpful in preparing me for my career. But I received most of my training in the Air Force.

"The best part of this job is knowing that we can help save lives and property."

Meteorologist

Weather observer

You may have heard the expression, "Everyone talks about the weather, but no one does anything about it." Although we cannot change the weather, some people try to observe, understand, and predict it.

A **meteorologist** studies weather information from weather stations, balloons, satellites, and radar. He or she uses the information to make a forecast.

Radio and television stations often hire meteorologists. Airports also need meteorologists. They let pilots know what kind of weather to expect along the flight route. Meteorologists who work for the National Weather Service receive information from hurricane hunters.

Meteorology students study math and science in college.

**Climatologists** are meteorologists who do not predict the everyday weather. Instead, they study the yearly patterns of the weather and make forecasts for the next year, ten years, or even hundred years.

**Weather observers** provide information to meteorologists. They watch the sky for changes in the clouds and use instruments to record the weather conditions. Weather observers learn how to use these instruments during one or two years in college.

To handle all the information that comes in from weather stations, a meteorologist depends on a computer and a **computer operator.** The computer operator stores information on computer tapes. The operator may program the computer to use the information to make forecasts. People who want to be computer operators usually go to a computer-training school.

# On Your Own

## Picture Clue

The photograph on the first page of this unit is a kind of storm that begins over warm, ocean water. The storm's whirling clouds bring heavy rains and strong winds. These storms cause damage along the coasts of the Gulf of Mexico and Atlantic Ocean.

## Projects

1. Record the weather in your area every day for one month. Include the temperature, amount of cloudiness, wind speed and direction, and air pressure. Be sure you record the weather *at the same time* each day.

2. Make a wind vane using a plastic straw and construction paper. Cut out a small arrow point and a large arrow tail from the paper. Glue the point and tail to the straw to make the shape of a wind vane similar to the one on page 46. Stick a pin through the straw and then through a pencil eraser. Your wind vane should be balanced and able to spin freely. Take your wind vane outside to tell from which direction the wind is coming.

3. Look in library books or an encyclopedia to find the usual number of tornadoes that occur in each state every year. Find the states that have the most and the fewest number of tornadoes. Report your findings to the class.

## Books About Science

*A January Fog Will Freeze a Hog and Other Weather Folklore* by Hubert Davis, ed. Crown, 1977. Learn about old sayings used to predict the weather. Is there any truth to these sayings? How did they start?

*Tornadoes, Killer Storms* by George Laycock. McKay, 1979. Learn more about tornadoes and what to do if one strikes.

*What's Happening to Our Weather?* by Daniel Cohen. M. Evans, 1979. Discover how our weather is changing and how people can control some of the weather.

# Unit Test

## Label the Drawing

Number your paper from 1–5. Next to each number, write the name of the instrument pictured beside that number. Then, write what the instrument measures.

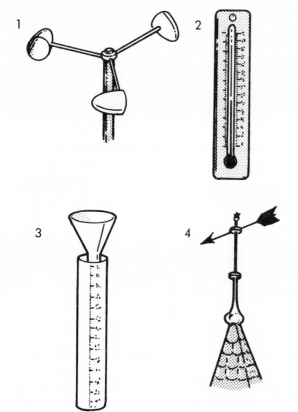

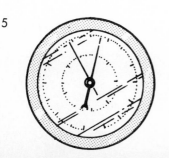

## Multiple Choice

Number your paper from 6–10. Next to each number, write the letter of the word or words that best complete the statement or answer the question.

6. Hurricanes form over
    a. cold land.
    b. cold water.
    c. warm land.
    d. warm water.

7. Temperature is affected by the
    a. amount of sunlight.
    b. type of surface.
    c. nearness to water.
    d. Answers a, b, and c are correct.

8. Cold air pushes under warm air at a
    a. warm front.
    b. cold front.
    c. warm air mass.
    d. cold air mass.

9. Along a warm front, you often find
    a. steady rain.
    b. tornadoes.
    c. the most violent thunderstorms.
    d. hurricanes.

10. The strongest winds on earth are found in a
    a. hurricane.
    b. stratus cloud.
    c. tornado.
    d. thunderstorm.

# UNIT THREE
# FORCES WITHIN THE EARTH

A quivering rumble
  beneath the ground
The shattering feeling
  all around

Becky Schumann *age 10*

# Chapter 5
# Inside the Earth

The huge crack shown in the picture traces a path through the island of Iceland. Sometimes melted rock oozes out of parts of the crack. The melted rock pushes against the walls of the crack and widens Iceland by about the width of your thumb every year.

The lessons in the chapter will describe what scientists think the inside of the earth is like. You will learn how the land beneath your feet moves and changes.

1 Making a Time Line

2 How Do We Use Land, Water, and Air?

3 What Is Inside the Earth?

4 Are the Continents Moving?

# 1 Making a Time Line

In history you learn about events that happened hundreds and thousands of years ago. When you study the earth, you often learn about events that happened millions or billions of years ago.

The canyon, shown here, has been forming for millions of years. The earth is thought to be about 4,500 million—or 4.5 billion—years old. These numbers are hard to imagine. Making time lines will give you a better idea of long periods of time.

First, cut a strip of paper about 3 centimeters wide and 1 meter long. The length of this paper stands for 1,000 years. Each millimeter stands for 1 year. Next, mark this year's date at one end of the paper. Now, use a ruler to mark the following events on your time line: your birth date, first moonwalk (1969), Columbus's first voyage to America (1492).

Get another strip of paper 1 meter long. This time, each millimeter stands for 1,000 years. The length of the whole strip stands for 1,000,000 years. Mark the year 2000 at the far right of the paper strip. Now, mark the following events on your time line: Roman Empire (2,000 years ago), Great Lakes formed (11,000 years ago), saber-toothed cats lived (500,000 years ago).

## Think About It

1. Could you mark on your second time line an event that happened 200 million years ago? Why?
2. **Challenge** How many million-year time lines would you have to tape end to end to show the entire history of the earth?

Canyon is millions of years old

81

# 2 How Do We Use Land, Water, and Air?

## Have You Heard?
Although New York City is near the Atlantic Ocean, the city gets drinking water from lakes more than 160 km away.

When astronauts in space look at the earth, they notice many things about the planet. They see the brown and dark green colors of the continents. They notice the deep blue color of the oceans and white clouds whirling across the earth. They also see a thin, blue glow covering the whole planet.

An astronaut in space sees the three major parts of the earth—land, water, and air. Only about one-fourth of the earth's surface is land. Most of the land is divided into seven continents, as the map shows. We work, play, live, and grow most of our food on land. But we could not do any of these things without water.

Without water, life could not exist. Three-fourths of the earth is covered with water. But most of this water is salty ocean water. We cannot drink salt water without becoming sick. Most of the water we use for drinking and washing comes from lakes, rivers, and underground streams.

Blue glow of atmosphere

Notice the thin, blue glow above the earth's surface. This glow is the earth's air—or **atmosphere.** The atmosphere is a mixture of gases. Plants and animals need some of these gases to live. When you look up at a blue sky, you are seeing the atmosphere from the inside out.

Land, water, and air affect each other. For example, water evaporating from oceans makes the air moist. Moisture in the air affects the weather and climate. The weather and climate of an area affect the land and the plants that grow there.

**atmosphere** (at′mə sfir), the air surrounding the earth.

## Think About It

1. Name the three major parts of the earth.
2. Why is water in lakes important to us?
3. **Challenge** How would our planet be different if there were no atmosphere?

# 3 What Is Inside the Earth?

In the 1800s, Jules Verne wrote a book called *Journey to the Center of the Earth*. During the journey, Professor Lidenbrock and his friends face many adventures. Some adventures in the book could happen. But you will learn why such a journey might be impossible.

The earth is shaped like a ball—or **sphere.** Long ago, people wondered what the inside of this sphere was like. As people dug mines and wells, they found out more about the earth. The mine in the picture goes hundreds of meters into the earth. The deepest well in the world goes down about 9 kilometers. But the center of the earth is almost 6,400 kilometers down. How can we find out about the inside of the earth without seeing it?

**sphere** (sfir), round object shaped like a ball.

## Find Out

Use the *Guinness Book of World Records* to find the name and location of the deepest mine in the world.

Deep mine

When you throw a stone into a pond, waves spread out from the splash. Just as the stone causes water waves, earthquakes and underground explosions cause waves in the earth. The waves travel through the earth in all directions.

Scientists use instruments to measure the speed and direction of the waves inside the earth. They know how fast waves travel through solid rock. They also know that some waves stop when they run into melted rock. Scientists observe the waves to figure out—or infer—about the inside of the earth.

Scientists think the earth is divided into three major layers, as shown. You can compare them to the layers of a peach.

The outside layer—or **crust**—is thin like the skin of the peach. The crust is made of solid rock about 40 kilometers thick. Mines and wells are dug into this layer.

You can compare the second layer—the **mantle**—to the yellow part of the peach that you eat. Most of the mantle is solid rock. It is about 2,800 kilometers thick. But a thin layer in the upper mantle is made of softer, partly melted rock.

The center of the earth—the **core**—is like the pit—or seed—of the peach. The center of the core is mostly solid iron. This solid iron is surrounded by a layer of melted iron. Temperatures in the core are thought to be as high as 5,500° Celsius—the temperature of the sun's surface.

**crust,** thin, outer layer of the earth.

**mantle** (man′tl), thick layer of the earth, beneath the crust.

**core** (kôr), center part of the earth, beneath the mantle.

## Think About It

1. Write two sentences to briefly describe each layer of the earth.
2. **Challenge** What would be some problems in trying to travel to the center of the earth?

# Activity

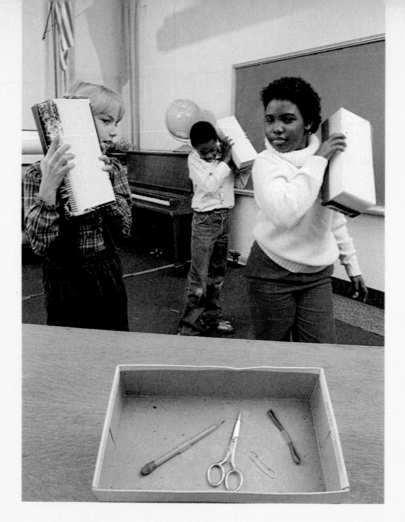

## Investigating Mystery Boxes

### Purpose
To describe the contents of a box without looking inside.

### You Will Need
• covered shoe box containing several objects
• tape

### Directions
1. Ask your teacher for a covered shoe box.
2. Tilt, turn, and shake the box. Observe how the objects in the box move. Do they roll or slide? Are they heavy or light? Observe how the objects sound when they hit the sides of the box. On a piece of paper, write the names of the objects you think are in the box.
3. Open the box to see how well you did.
4. Make up a mystery box for your partner. Use 2 objects from the collection your teacher has provided. Be sure your partner cannot see which objects you choose.
5. Give the covered box to your partner, and repeat steps 2 and 3.
6. Try another way to discover what is in the box. While you look away, ask your partner to arrange and tape 4 objects in the box, as shown in the picture.
7. Without looking in the box, draw a map of the objects by feeling them.
8. Compare your map to the objects in the box.

### Think About It
1. In step 2, how did you and your partner discover what was in the box?
2. **Challenge** What could you *not* tell about the objects by shaking or by feeling them?

# Discover!

## Digging for the Past

What was the earth like 150 million years ago? Think how hard it is to answer that question. No person was around to keep records. How can we find out what happened that long ago?

Some clues about the ancient past come from deep beneath the oceans. Scientists study cores, which are long pieces of rock taken from the ocean bottom. Cores are made by sinking a hollow drill into the earth's crust below the ocean. The drill fills with rock as it goes deeper into the crust. Then, the drill is pulled back up and opened. When scientists observe the core they are looking at rock that no one else has ever seen!

The things found in a core tell a great deal about the earth's history. Many cores contain fossils—the remains of dead organisms from the past. Fossils are clues to the age of the rocks in a core. Scientists know about how long ago many of these fossils lived. When scientists see a fossil in a rock, they know the rock formed about the same time the fossil died.

Each core taken from the ocean bottom provides a quick look into history. The more cores scientists study, the better they can read earth history.

Collecting cores is not an easy job. Drilling on the ocean bottom is far more difficult than drilling on dry land. The drill has to go to the bottom of the ocean before it even begins drilling into the crust.

A special kind of ship is needed to do this research. The *Glomar Challenger,* shown in the picture, is such a ship. In 12 years it has made more than 80 trips and collected cores from every ocean.

With the help of people aboard ships like the *Glomar Challenger,* we are discovering more about the earth's past.

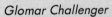
*Glomar Challenger*

# 4 Are the Continents Moving?

Look at the map of the continents. Many of them seem to fit together like pieces of a giant jigsaw puzzle. Most scientists think the continents were once joined in one large chunk of land. They think the continents broke apart and are still moving!

Scientists have found clues that seem to show the continents move. The remains of a certain kind of animal were found in South America and in Africa. Animals of this kind do not live today. The drawings on the map show where the remains were found. These animals could not cross the ocean between Africa and South America. But if Africa and South America were once joined, the animals could have moved from continent to continent.

Continental jigsaw puzzle

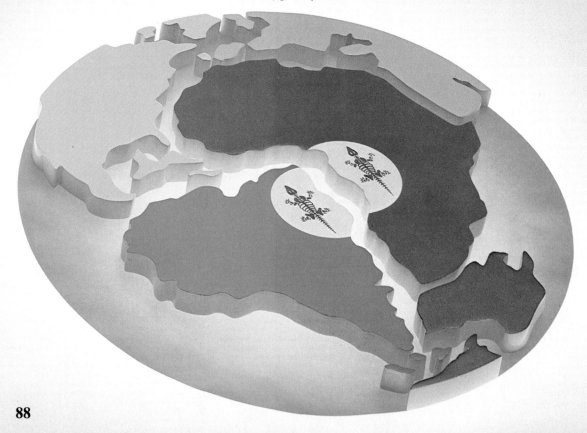

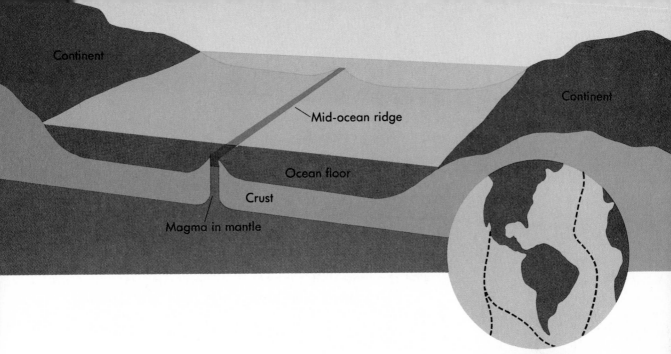

Continent

Mid-ocean ridge

Continent

Ocean floor

Crust

Magma in mantle

In the 1960s, scientists found stronger evidence that continents move. Scientists exploring the ocean floors made some strange discoveries. They found a long chain of underwater mountains in the middle of the Atlantic Ocean! The tops of these mountains were about 2 kilometers below the ocean's surface. This underwater mountain chain—or **mid-ocean ridge**—is 65,000 kilometers long. The drawings on the right show how the mountains run through the oceans of the world.

Notice above that the ridge in the Atlantic Ocean is really two mountain chains side by side. A long valley lies between the mountain chains. The floor of the valley has many large cracks. Melted rock—or **magma**—rises out of these cracks. The magma rises from the mantle. When the magma comes out onto the ocean floor, it hardens and forms new crust. The new crust piles up to make mountains. The crust slowly moves away on both sides of the valley, allowing more magma to come up. The continents move because the crust moves.

**mid-ocean ridge,** underwater mountain chain where new crust is forming.

**magma** (mag′mə), melted rock inside the earth.

## Have You Heard?
Scientists think the Atlantic Ocean has been spreading and growing for 200 million years. The Atlantic Ocean is still growing.

## What Are Plates?

When the crust moves, all the earth's crust does not move at once. It slowly moves in sections called **plates.** Each plate includes the crust and part of the mantle. Most plates are large and may be the size of a whole continent or ocean. The plates move at different times, at different speeds, and in different directions. The mid-ocean ridge is the boundary between two plates that are moving away from each other.

The drawing shows a boundary between two plates that bump into each other. Notice how one plate bends down deep into the mantle. Here, the plate melts.

**plate,** large section of the earth's crust that slowly moves.

### Think About It

1. What is happening at the mid-ocean ridge?
2. What are plates?
3. **Challenge** Part of the mid-ocean ridge runs through the Red Sea. What may be happening to the Red Sea?

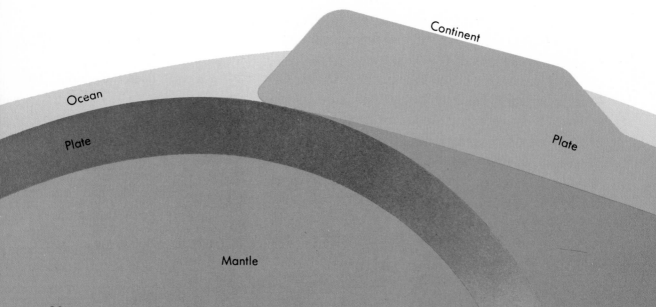

Continent

Ocean

Plate

Plate

Mantle

# Tie It Together

## Sum It Up

1. Letter your paper a–e. Next to each letter, write the word that best completes each sentence below.

a. About one-fourth of the earth's surface is ▦ .

b. The earth's air is called the ▦ .

c. Scientists study ▦ to infer about the inside of the earth.

d. Mines and wells are dug into the earth's ▦ .

e. Most scientists think the ▦ were once joined.

2. The drawing below appears in the chapter. Letter your paper f–h. Label the drawings by writing the correct word next to each letter.

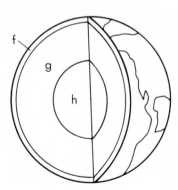

## Challenge!

1. Why does Los Angeles get most of its water from the Colorado River rather than from the Pacific Ocean?

2. Certain kinds of waves travel fast through solid rock but do not move at all through liquid. What do you think happens when the waves run into partly-melted rock?

3. How could you get an idea of how deep a pit is without actually looking into it?

4. Suppose a scientist finds the remains of palm trees in northern Canada. The remains are millions of years old. How might this discovery be a clue that the continents moved?

5. On the ocean floor, where would you look to find the youngest rocks? The oldest rocks?

## Science Words

atmosphere

core

crust

magma

mantle

mid-ocean ridge

plate

sphere

# Chapter 6
# Building and Shaking the Earth

On February 20, 1943, a Mexican farmer went to work in his fields. The sky was clear over the village of Paricutín. Late in the afternoon the farmer heard a low rumble. He saw a column of smoke only 6 centimeters wide rising from a small hole in the ground. Three hours later, the hole was a pit 10 meters across. Clouds of ash billowed from the pit. Red-hot stones were thrown into the air. The low rumble grew into a terrifying noise. The next day, in place of the pit stood a hill 12 meters high! A volcano was born! During the next 9 years it grew over 400 meters above the farmer's ruined fields.

The lessons in this chapter describe how changes in the earth's crust cause earthquakes and volcanoes.

# 1 Modeling Earth's Forces

Whenever you push against or pull on an object, you use force. You use force to push a tack into a wooden board. If you use a machine, such as a hammer, you make the force greater.

But forces and pressures inside the earth are much greater than any machine can make. Forces within the earth push and pull on the earth's crust. You can build a model to show what forces can do to the crust.

Flatten three pieces of clay. The flat pieces of clay stand for layers of rock in the earth's crust. Stack and press the layers on top of one another, as shown. What do you think will happen to the layers when you push against opposite sides of the clay? Now, slowly push against the clay, as shown. Observe what happens to the clay.

## Think About It

1. What happened to the clay when you pressed against it?
2. **Challenge** What can forces in the earth do to the crust?

Gently press layers

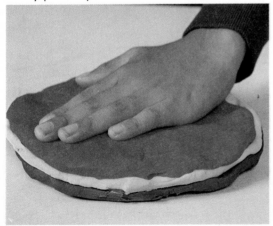

Push against clay

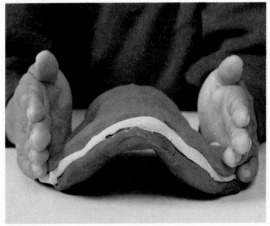

# 2 What Are Faults?

The pavement in the picture is very strong. But most paved streets, sidewalks, and playgrounds have cracks. Pressure from under the ground causes some of the cracks. For example, a tree root might grow under a sidewalk. The growing root presses against the sidewalk and can crack it, as shown.

When you press against clay, it bends and changes shape. As you add more pressure, cracks form in the clay. Pressure in the earth's crust also causes cracks. If the rock in the crust moves or slides along a crack, the crack is called a **fault.** The drawing shows a fault. Notice how the land moved along the crack.

Rock along a fault can remain still for hundreds or thousands of years. Pressure may build up during this time. When the pressure reaches a certain point, it forces the rock to slide. The rock along a fault can move 10 to 15 meters in just a few seconds.

Trees can crack sidewalks

**fault,** crack in the earth that rock moves along.

## Have You Heard?

Faults are many different lengths. Some are only a few cm long. Other faults are over 1,000 km long—longer than California!

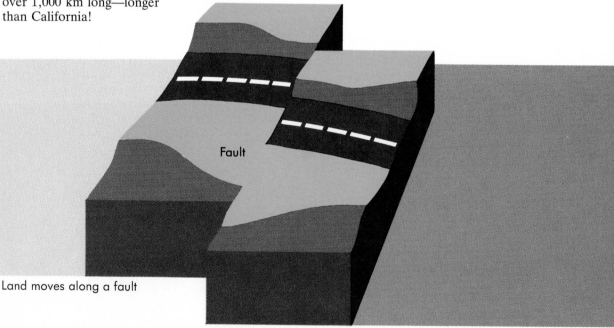

Fault

Land moves along a fault

San Andreas Fault

Fence broken by land movement

Many faults are deep in the crust. We cannot see them. But some faults are visible on the earth's surface. The drawing below shows how land along a fault rose to form a cliff.

Sometimes land along a fault moves from side to side instead of up and down. The land along the San Andreas Fault in California has moved from side to side. The arrow on the picture shows how land on one side of the fault moves north. Notice what happened to a fence that runs across the fault. As the land moved, it carried part of the fence with it.

Rocks in the crust push together, pull apart, or rub against each other where the earth's plates meet. Therefore, many plate boundaries are faults. The San Andreas Fault is part of the boundary between two plates.

## Find Out
Explain how a fault can cause a waterfall.

## Think About It

1. What causes a fault?
2. What causes many faults to form at plate boundaries?
3. **Challenge** What might happen to a river that crosses the San Andreas Fault?

95

# 3 What Causes Earthquakes?

## Have You Heard?

In ancient times, people made up stories to explain earthquakes. One story said that the earth rested on the back of a giant bull. When the bull moved, the earth shook.

You can hear a low rumble as a train approaches a railroad crossing. As the train's heavy engine passes, the ground shakes beneath your feet.

When huge blocks of rock move along a fault, the ground also shakes. An earthquake takes place. The shaking often causes the ground to crack. But the earth does not open up and swallow things. Most cracks are only a few meters deep.

Earthquakes usually take place at faults that are near plate boundaries. Many earthquakes occur near the San Andreas Fault.

## How Do Earthquakes Affect Us?

Most earthquakes are so weak, people cannot feel them. Other earthquakes rattle dishes and windows. A few earthquakes are strong enough to knock down buildings and destroy entire towns.

A strong earthquake took place in southern Italy in 1980. A large fault near southern Italy is at the boundary between 2 plates. One chilly November evening the plates moved slightly past each other. This movement caused Europe's worst earthquake in 65 years. The picture shows some of the destruction. Walls of buildings shook and fell to the ground. Thousands of people were killed. In less than 1 minute, more than 100 towns crumbled!

People have several ways to describe the strength of an earthquake. The numbers in the table below refer to damage done by an earthquake. The earthquake in Italy measured 9.

| **Damage scale of earthquakes** | |
| --- | --- |
| I | Not felt by people |
| II | Felt by a few people on the upper floors of buildings |
| III | Felt by a great number of people |
| IV | Feels like passing of heavy truck; dishes rattle |
| V | Furniture shakes; pictures on walls move |
| VI | People awakened from sleep; trees shake |
| VII | Windows break; walls crack |
| VIII | Chimneys and steeples fall; rocks fall from mountains |
| IX | Total destruction of buildings; the ground cracks |
| X | Bridges damaged or destroyed; landslides occur; water thrown on the banks of lakes |
| XI | Railroad tracks twist; dams break |
| XII | Everything made by people is destroyed; the land changes shape; new faults form; rivers change their direction of flow |

## Can We Predict Earthquakes?

If we could predict earthquakes, many lives would be saved. People would have time to go to safe places, away from falling buildings.

Scientists around the world are trying to learn how to predict earthquakes. They think certain things may happen before an earthquake strikes. The ground may bulge near a fault. The water level in a well near a fault may suddenly change. A number of small earthquakes—or **tremors**—could mean a strong earthquake is coming. Some scientists think animals behave strangely before an earthquake.

Scientists use many instruments to help them read the "signs" of a coming earthquake. The instrument being used in the picture measures the slightest bulge or change in the shape of the land.

In 1975, Chinese scientists predicted a strong earthquake 24 hours before it happened. The signs began in 1974. Tremors occurred throughout a large part of China. Water levels in wells rose and fell. Animals acted strange. Then, in early February of 1975, the tremors happened more often. Scientists held an emergency meeting. They warned the people that a strong earthquake would probably strike within 2 days. People left their homes to stay in open fields. The next day, a powerful earthquake destroyed almost every building in the area. However, the prediction probably saved about 100,000 lives!

**tremor** (trem′ər), small earthquake that usually does not cause much damage.

Measuring change in land

## Think About It

1. What causes an earthquake?
2. List three "signs" used to predict earthquakes.
3. **Challenge** Why do earthquakes often happen in California?

# Do You Know?

## Animals Might Predict Earthquakes

Birds scatter

Dogs howl and run in circles. Snakes crawl out of their holes. Fish jump above water surfaces. Farm animals try to escape from barns. What is happening? According to some people, an earthquake may be coming!

Some scientists think certain animals can sense a coming earthquake days or hours before it happens. In some cases animal behavior has been successful in helping predict earthquakes.

Before the Chinese earthquake in February, 1975, people observed strange animal behavior. Birds suddenly flew away, as shown, and would not return to their nests. Chickens refused to enter their coops. Rats scampered around, bumping into things. Well-trained police dogs howled, would not obey commands, and kept sniffing the ground.

What might these animals know that we do not? Perhaps they can sense some of the changes that happen in the earth before an earthquake. Some scientists think certain animals can hear low booms that come before an earthquake. Perhaps they can smell certain gases that escape from the earth before an earthquake.

To study the possible connection between animals and earthquakes, scientists in California set up "Project Earthquake Watch." The project ran from 1979 to 1982 and included over 1,000 volunteers throughout California. The volunteers observed animals and called the project headquarters every day to report on their animals' behavior.

During the project, 13 earthquakes were recorded near where the animals were being observed. The volunteers observed an unusually high amount of strange animal behavior before 7 of these earthquakes!

Because of the efforts of scientists and volunteers around the world, we will someday know if we can depend on animals to warn us against these disasters.

# 4 How Do Volcanoes Form?

**lava,** melted rock or magma that comes out onto the surface of the earth.

**eruption** (i rup′shən), the bursting forth of material from a volcano.

When thick, gray smoke rises from a house, you know something is happening. The house is on fire. When smoke or ash rises from a volcano, you know something is happening deep inside the earth.

The inside of the earth is hot enough to melt rock. The drawing shows a pocket of melted rock—magma—deep underground. Pressure squeezes the magma up through the crust just as you squeeze toothpaste through a tube. Sometimes the magma breaks through to the surface and makes an opening.

Magma that comes out onto the surface of the earth is called **lava.** During an **eruption,** lava, gases, rocks, and ashes burst from the opening. After many eruptions, lava, rocks, and ash build a mountain called a volcano.

The shape of a volcano depends on what came out during the eruptions. The volcano on the left was built from rocks and ash but very little lava. The volcano on the right is mostly lava. Lava oozed out of the opening time after time. The lava spread out from the opening like thick syrup. It hardened to form the shape of an upside-down saucer.

Volcano made of rocks and ash

Volcano made of lava

Magma

Pressure

Mount St. Helens erupting

## How Do Volcanoes Affect Us?

When a volcano erupts (i rupts′), it is deadly to all living things nearby. The force of the blast from Mount St. Helens, shown here, knocked down trees for 500 kilometers around. Hot, choking ash killed many animals and some people. Ash destroyed or damaged crops hundreds of kilometers to the east.

Volcanoes are also helpful in some ways. After many years, hardened lava changes into dark soil, which makes good farmland. Some countries, such as the United States, Japan, and Italy, are learning to use heat from volcanoes to make electricity.

### Think About It

1. How does a volcano form?
2. Describe the shape of a volcano built from lava.
3. **Challenge** How could ash from Mount St. Helens affect crops hundreds of kilometers to the east?

## Have You Heard?

When lava is thrown into the air, it often hardens before hitting the ground.

## Find Out

How did the Hawaiian Islands form?

# 5 How Do Mountains Build Up?

**fault-block mountain,** mountain that is formed when a block of land rises and tilts along a fault.

**dome mountain,** mountain that is formed when magma rises and pushes the land up.

Dome mountain

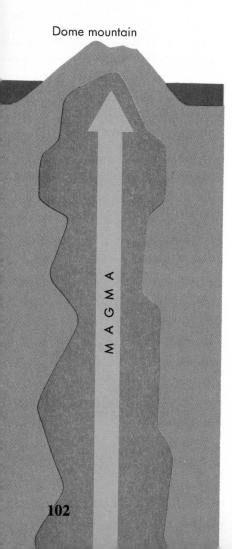

What do you think of when you hear the word mountain? Some people imagine snow-covered peaks. Others picture round, tree-covered hills.

Mountains form when the land rises or builds up. Volcanoes are mountains that build up from lava, rocks, and ash.

Some mountains appear when land rises along a fault. The drawing shows how the Teton Mountains grew. A large block of land slowly rose and tilted along a fault. Mountains of this kind are **fault-block mountains.** Notice how the tilt makes one side of the mountains steeper than the other side.

The drawing on the left shows another kind of mountain. Magma sometimes acts like a fist pushing up toward the surface of the earth. Pressure from the magma pushes the rocks up into a dome. This kind of mountain is a **dome mountain.** In time, the magma hardens into solid rock.

Fault-block mountains

The Himalaya Mountains in Asia are the tallest mountains in the world. They are forming where two plates are colliding. As the plates move toward each other, the land is squeezed and crumpled, as in the drawing. Mountains such as these are called **folded mountains.** The Himalaya Mountains will continue to grow as long as the plates push against each other.

**folded mountain,** mountain that is formed where the land is folded and crumpled at a plate boundary.

## Think About It

1. List four ways mountains form.
2. Why are the Himalaya Mountains still growing?
3. **Challenge** Two plates are colliding on the west side of South America. What kind of mountains would you expect to find here? Name them.

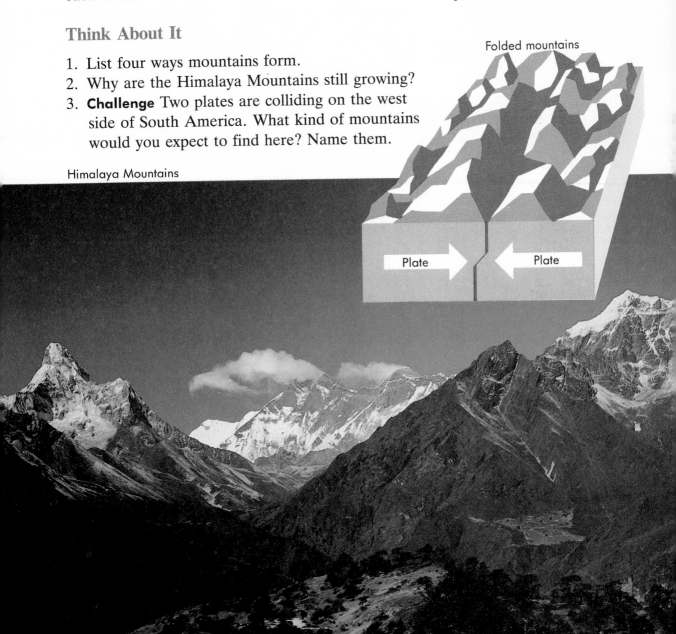

Folded mountains

Plate     Plate

Himalaya Mountains

# Activity

## Making a Model of a Dome Mountain

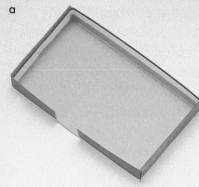
a

### Purpose
To make a model showing how dome mountains form.

### You Will Need
- cardboard shoe-box lid
- damp sand
- round balloon
- plastic straw
- small piece of clay
- scissors
- tape

### Directions
1. Cut a notch into one of the sides of the shoe-box lid, as in *a*.
2. Fill the bottom of the lid with a thin layer of damp sand.
3. Place the straw inside the balloon. Tape the balloon around the straw, as in *b*.
4. Lay the balloon in the lid, as in *c*.
5. Put another layer of damp sand in the lid. Make sure the balloon is covered.

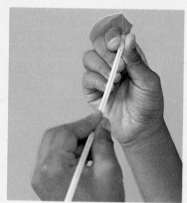
b

c

6. Slowly blow into the balloon through the straw. Observe what happens to the sand.
7. Stop blowing when most of the balloon breaks through the sand.
8. Seal the straw with the piece of clay so that air does not leave the balloon.
9. Make a side-view drawing of your dome model. In your picture, draw the sand around the balloon.

### Think About It
1. What happened to the sand as you blew up the balloon?
2. What does the sand in your model represent?
3. What does the balloon in your model represent?
4. **Challenge** As a dome mountain forms, what do you think might happen to the top layers of rocks?

# Tie It Together

## Sum It Up

The following is an imaginary newspaper report of an earthquake. Label your paper from 1–10. Finish the story by filling the numbered blanks. Write the correct word from the list below next to each number on your paper.

ash            plates
bulge          predicted
earthquake     safe
fault          tremors
lava           volcano

Yesterday, the country of Peru suffered its worst __(1)__ in twenty years. The earthquake took place when two blocks of land on either side of a __(2)__ slid past each other. There are many faults on the west coast of South America. Here, two of the earth's __(3)__ push against each other to form the Andes Mountains.

Besides the earthquake, some people reported the eruption of a __(4)__. Eyewitnesses said a river of __(5)__ flowed down the north side of the volcano and destroyed two farms. Clouds of hot __(6)__ were blown across the mountains by a strong west wind.

The earthquake also caused destruction, leveling seven towns. But few people were hurt because scientists recently __(7)__ this earthquake. Two weeks ago, scientists noticed a slight __(8)__ in the ground near one of the faults. Last week, small earthquakes, or __(9)__, shook the countryside. Yesterday, the people were asked to leave their towns and to set up camps in open fields. Today, the buildings are gone, but the people are __(10)__.

## Challenge!

1. Are all cracks in the earth called faults? Explain your answer.

2. Look at a map of California. Some scientists say that, millions of years from now, Los Angeles will be next to San Francisco. How could this statement be true?

3. Many volcanoes are in southern Alaska, where two plates meet. What two other things might you expect to find in southern Alaska? Explain your answers.

4. Explain how you could use two sheets of paper to show how the Himalaya Mountains formed.

## Science Words

dome mountain

eruption

fault

fault-block mountain

folded mountain

lava

tremor

# Laboratory

## Forces Acting on Objects

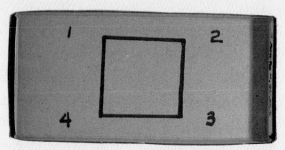

*a*

### Purpose
To observe how the shape of a building can determine how well the building keeps from falling when forces act on it.

### You Will Need
• cardboard shoe-box lid
• centimeter ruler
• 2 books
• 30 sugar cubes

### Stating the Problem
Suppose you heard that an earthquake was about to strike. Would you be safe in a tall, narrow building that was not well supported? Might some buildings be safer than others?

### Investigating the Problem

*Part I*
1. In the center of a shoe-box lid, draw a square that is 10 cm long on each side. Number the corners of

*b*

the square *1* through *4* as shown in picture *a*.
2. Place the lid across the sides of 2 books as shown in picture *b*.
3. Build a sugar-cube "building" on each corner of the square. Picture *c* shows the kinds of buildings you should make.
4. Use your fingers in a flicking motion to strike

under the center of the square, as shown in picture *d*.
5. Record which buildings are still in place after you strike the lid.
6. Strike the lid again with greater force. If all the buildings have not toppled, continue striking the lid until all the buildings have toppled or broken apart.

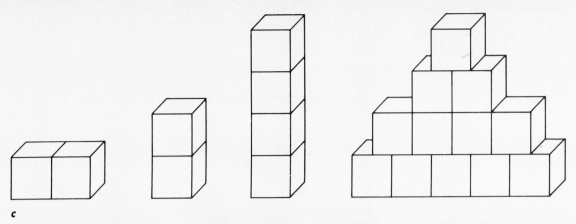

c

## Part II

1. On one of the 4 corners of the square, build a sugar-cube building that is at least 4 sugar cubes high. Design the building so it does not topple when you strike under the lid. You may use all 30 sugar cubes for the building.

## Making Conclusions

1. What force acted on the sugar-cube buildings?
2. Which building toppled the soonest? Why?
3. Using your observations of the sugar-cube buildings, what do you think might happen to real buildings during an earthquake?
4. How did you design your building so it would not topple when a force acted on it?

d

# Careers

### Geologist

As a boy, David did a lot of camping with his family. On these trips he became interested in why the earth's surface looks the way it does. So, what did he do about this interest? "I became a geologist," says David. "Now I can answer a lot of the questions I had as a young boy.

"I do a lot of detective work. To a trained eye, rivers, rocks, and other features are clues to what happened in the past. Geologists can also put the clues together to predict what might happen in the future."

For the past few years David has been studying the San Andreas Fault in California. "Part of my job was to map the area in Los Angeles County where earthquakes often occur. The map shows the places where earthquakes might happen. People can use this map to avoid building homes in high-risk areas.

"In helping to make the map, I looked at pictures of the area taken from the air. I also studied work done by other geologists. Then, I headed outside to study the faults and rocks.

After much careful observation, other workers and I put together the map."

Eventually, David, and those who work with him, would like to be able to predict earthquakes.

To become a geologist, or any other scientist, a person usually goes to school for a few years after college. But going to school has never bothered David. "As a scientist I have been learning new things all my life. Whether I am in a classroom, in my office, or in a canyon, I always think of myself as a student."

People in many jobs work with the materials from the earth. Some people study these materials, while others mine the materials for people to use.

Taking temperatures seems like a pretty easy job to do. But what about taking the temperature of an active volcano? This exciting and dangerous task is one part of a **volcanologist's** (vol′kə nol′ə jist) job. These scientists are geologists who study the insides of volcanoes. They collect lava and gas samples from volcanoes. One of their most important jobs is to try to predict when volcanoes will erupt.

A **seismologist** (sīz mol′ə jist) is a geologist who studies earthquakes. In some places builders talk to seismologists before they decide where to construct buildings.

To become a geologist of any kind, you need to take geology, math, and physics classes in college.

When geologists go on field explorations, they are usually joined by a **geology technician.** This person helps the geologist in the field. A technician often runs equipment, makes maps, or takes rock samples. The technician may also take notes that the geologist uses later.

Technicians study earth science for two years at a college. They also get on-the-job training.

While geologists study materials in the earth, **miners** remove the materials from the earth. Mines may be dug to remove rock, coal, metal, or salt. A miner may drive trucks, drill through rock, or handle explosives.

One of the most important things we take from the inside of the earth is oil. A **drilling-crew worker** helps run the machinery that drills deep into the earth's crust for oil. Many workers have jobs on huge platforms in the ocean, where much oil is being drilled.

Miners and drillers learn from other workers on the job. But they should have at least a high-school education. Some workers take classes to learn how to run special machines.

Volcanologist

Miner

Drilling crew worker

# On Your Own

## Picture Clue

The photograph on the first page of this unit shows what happens when melted rock from inside the earth rises to the surface. This melted rock often hardens and piles up to make a certain kind of mountain.

## Projects

1. Use library books to find out about the Alaska earthquake of 1964. Report your findings to the class.

2. Build a model volcano using clay or plaster of Paris. You can use baking soda and vinegar to make the eruption. Library books will show you different ways to make your model.

3. Pretend you are a reporter. Write an imaginary newspaper story about an earthquake or an erupting volcano. Include the time, date, and place it happens. You can also use imaginary names of people. Draw a picture to go with your story.

## Books About Science

*Earthquake* by John Gabriel Navarra. Doubleday, 1980. Find out more about earthquakes and earthquake predictions. How have people learned to live with earthquakes in their area?

*Global Jigsaw Puzzle* by Irene Kiefer. Atheneum, 1978. Learn more about plates and moving continents. How did these ideas come about?

*Volcanoes* by Susan Harris. Watts, 1979. Learn more about volcanoes, the different kinds of eruptions, and how volcanoes form.

# Unit Test

## True or False

Number your paper from 1–5. Next to each number, write *true* if the sentence is correct and *false* if the sentence is incorrect. Make each false statement true by changing the underlined word or words and writing the correct word or words on your paper.

1. Most of the earth's water is found in rivers.

2. A fracture is a crack in the earth that rocks move along.

3. Earthquakes are caused by huge blocks of rock moving along a fault.

4. New crust is forming at the mid-ocean ridge.

5. Folded mountains form when land rises and tilts along a fault.

## Matching

Number your paper from 6–10. Read the description in Column I. Next to each number, write the letter of the word or words from Column II that best match the description in Column I.

**Column I**

6. mountain formed from eruptions of lava, rocks, and ashes

7. thin, outside layer of the earth

8. sections of the earth's crust that move

9. center of the earth, made mostly of iron

10. places where most earthquakes occur

**Column II**

a. crust

b. core

c. volcano

d. near plate boundaries

e. plates

# UNIT FOUR
# CHANGES IN THE EARTH'S SURFACE

Shapes on the mountains
  of living things
The shapes watch over
  the changing earth.

Dana Jose *age 9*

# Chapter 7
# Agents of Change

You might think the earth's surface is something that never changes. After all, much of the surface is solid rock. But, every day, the surface changes a little bit. Even now, pieces of rock are breaking apart. Trees, such as the one shown, are breaking rocks. Some rocks are tumbling down hills. Some are flowing through streams. Other rocks are staying in place, crumbling into smaller and smaller pieces.

The lessons in this chapter will show you how the earth's surface is changing every day. These changes form soil, rivers, and other things you often see.

1 Observing a Drop of Water

2 What Is Weathering?

3 What Is Erosion?

4 How Can People Help Control Erosion?

# 1 Observing a Drop of Water

When rabbits dig holes in a field, they change the shape of the earth's surface. A few holes do not change the surface very much. But if the rabbits spend a week just digging holes, the field looks very different. Over a period of time, something small can make a big change in the shape of the land. Even drops of water can change the land.

Place a small mound of sand on a piece of waxed paper. Then, using a medicine dropper, let a drop of water fall on the sand, as shown. Observe the drop carefully. Now, hold the medicine dropper higher above the sand, and let another drop fall. Repeat the activity in several places on the mound.

Fill the medicine dropper again. Now, squirt all the water in one place on the sand. Refill the medicine dropper several times, squirting all the water in the same place.

## Think About It

1. What did one drop of water do to the sand mound?
2. What happened when you let a lot of water fall quickly on the sand in the same place?
3. **Challenge** How could a heavy rainfall change the earth's surface?

# 2 What Is Weathering?

weathering, the breaking down of rock.

frost action, the breaking apart of rocks by freezing water pushing against the sides of cracks in rocks.

Pressure

Frost action breaks rocks

## Have You Heard?

Unfortunately, the Great Sphinx has been weathered by people as well as by natural processes. In the 1700s a ruler ordered his soldiers to fire their guns at the nose of the Sphinx for target practice.

The Great Sphinx, shown below, is in Egypt. It was carved from rock over four thousand years ago. When the Sphinx was built, it was covered with white plaster and painted in bright colors. You can see what has happened to it since that time.

The painted plaster and much of the rock of the Sphinx have crumbled and worn away. The breaking down—or **weathering**—of rock happens every day all around the world. Rock can weather in many ways.

Notice the cracks in the rock shown in the drawing. Water from rain or melting snow often fills the cracks. As the water freezes, it takes up more space and pushes against the rock, as the arrows show. If melting and freezing continue, pieces of rock can break off. This type of weathering is called **frost action.** Frost action often causes potholes in roads, which make driving dangerous.

Plants also help weather rocks. Plants can grow in soil that collects in the cracks of rocks. As the roots grow, they push against the rock and weaken it. Sometimes the growing roots of a larger plant, such as a tree, can break a boulder apart.

Great Sphinx in Egypt

Cavern formed by weak acid eating away rock

Rocks are made up of **minerals**—nonliving, natural matter. Rainwater and gases in the air can change some minerals and cause rocks to weather.

One of the gases in the air is **carbon dioxide.** Plants need carbon dioxide to grow. But when this gas mixes with water, such as rain, a weak acid forms. This acid does not hurt us. But it slowly eats away at some minerals in rocks. The acid turns the hard minerals into a soft clay, and the rock slowly breaks apart. Sometimes the acid totally eats away the minerals and leaves a hollow space. Some of these hollow spaces are beautiful underground caverns, such as the one shown.

Some minerals contain iron. **Oxygen**—another gas in the air—combines with iron to make rust. You often see reddish-brown rust on an iron nail left outside. If the nail has totally weathered into rust, you can easily crumble it in your hand. Many kinds of rocks have iron that weathers into rust. This rust gives some rocks their gold and red colors.

**mineral** (min′ər əl), nonliving, natural matter that makes up rocks.

**carbon dioxide** (kär′bən dī ok′sīd), a colorless gas in the air that plants need in order to grow.

**oxygen** (ok′sə jən), a colorless gas in the air that all plants and animals need to live.

## How Does Weathering Help Us?

Weathering does much more than split and color rocks. As a large boulder weathers, it can break into many pieces. Each piece continues to weather into smaller and smaller pieces. In time, the pieces of rock get so small that they become **soil.** Soil comes from weathered rock and is needed to grow most of our food.

Although soil is mostly weathered rock, it is also made up of things that once lived. When plants and animals die, they rot—or decay—and become part of the soil. You may have seen a fallen tree, like this one, rotting in the forest. The tree is becoming part of the soil. The next time you pick up a handful of soil, you might be holding some of the remains of a tree and a mountain!

**soil,** tiny pieces of rock mixed with decayed organisms in which plants can grow.

## Think About It

1. List three ways in which rocks weather.
2. What is the most important result of weathering?
3. **Challenge** Why does frost action *not* work very well in places where the temperature is always below freezing?

### Have You Heard?
Decayed plants and animals give the top layers of soil its dark brown or black color.

Rotting tree becoming part of soil

# Do You Know?

## Weathering Causes Change

These stone pillars are about the same age. They were both carved in Egypt about 3,500 years ago. Yet, the two pillars look very different. The one on the left looks as though the sculptor finished it yesterday. The other pillar looks very worn. Can you explain the difference?

To solve this puzzle, you should know one more fact. One pillar has been in New York City's Central Park for over one hundred years. The other is still in Egypt. When the pillar was brought to New York, it began weathering much faster than it had in Egypt. Soon, many of the carved figures on the monument became hard to see.

What caused the New York pillar to weather faster than the Egyptian pillar? Part of the answer is the climate. The climate in Egypt is warm and dry. The climate in New York

Pillar in Egypt

Pillar in New York

includes hot and cold weather and a lot of rain and snow. Weathering takes place more quickly in a wet climate than in a dry climate.

The pillar has also weathered more quickly in New York because of air pollution. Any large city has a lot of factories and cars. The fuels people burn in factories and cars release

chemicals into the air. Some of these chemicals mix with moisture in the air to make weak acids. These acids slowly eat away at rock and speed up weathering.

Many people hope that we will find a way to save these monuments before all their historical carvings are weathered away.

# 3 What Is Erosion?

erosion (i rō′zhən), the wearing away and moving of materials by water, wind, and ice.

## Have You Heard?

Rivers that carry a great amount of soil often look brown and muddy, like parts of the Colorado River and the Mississippi River.

The running water in the picture is carrying the people along. But the water is carrying many other things besides the boat and people.

If you take a jar of water from a stream, you will see tiny pieces of soil in the water. Streams carry some soil, sand, or pebbles that were once part of the land. **Erosion** is the wearing away and moving of these materials by water, wind, and ice.

Water from many rainstorms caused erosion on this small hill. As raindrops rolled down the hill, they wore away—or eroded—the soil. You can see the paths that the water made as it carried the soil down the hill.

A fast-moving river can cause a lot of erosion. As water rubs against a riverbank, it wears away rocks as well as sand and soil. These materials flow along with the river.

Powerful running water

Erosion from rainstorms

Erosion along coast

Sand dunes moved into forest

You may have seen round pebbles in a stream. Most pebbles were larger rocks with rough edges when they first fell into the stream. But sand and stones in the stream kept banging against the rocks to form the smooth, round pebbles you often see.

Erosion also occurs along the coast. Large waves, splashing against the shore, formed the cliffs in the picture. Rocks and sand in the water crashed against the cliff and helped to erode it.

Wind also causes erosion. The wind can blow loose grains of soil and sand over a long distance. Wind is eroding the Great Sphinx in Egypt. First, weathering loosens the rock of the Sphinx. Then, sand blowing against the Sphinx acts like sandpaper to remove flakes of rock.

Wind erosion can blow sand into piles called sand dunes. Sand dunes form in deserts and along the shores of oceans and large lakes. Wind can continue to blow a sand dune across the land. In the picture, wind blew sand dunes from a beach into a forest.

Find Out

Use an encyclopedia to find out how much eroded material is carried into the Gulf of Mexico by the Mississippi River each year.

**121**

V-shaped valley

U-shaped valley

## How Does Ice Erode the Land?

Look at the two pictures of the valleys. The valley on the left is narrow and shaped like a **V.** The valley on the right also used to be V-shaped. But thousands of years ago it was filled with a huge amount of ice, called a **glacier.** As the glacier moved, it eroded the valley. Moving ice dug out the valley walls and floor. The glacier carried away rocks and soil. The valley became **U-shaped.**

**glacier** (glā′shər), a huge mass of ice that moves slowly and erodes the land.

### Think About It

1. What is erosion?
2. Explain how water, wind, and ice each cause erosion.
3. **Challenge** Explain why a rock with rough, sharp edges in a fast-moving stream probably has not been there very long.

# Activity

## Making a Model of Erosion

**Purpose**
To observe how moving water erodes rocks.

**You Will Need**
- 30 small, rough stones (all about the same size)
- 2 coffee cans with lids
- 2 large, clear plastic cups
- 3 sheets of paper towel
- masking tape
- marking pen

**Directions**
1. Ask your teacher for 30 stones, and place them in a pile.
2. Divide the pile into 3, with 10 stones in each pile. To do this, close your eyes and pick up the first stone you touch. Place it on a paper towel.
3. Each person in the group, with eyes closed, should take a turn picking up a stone until the 3 piles have 10 stones each.
4. Label the piles *A, B,* and *C.*
5. Put the stones from pile *A* into a can. Put the stones from pile *B* into the other can. Use the tape and pen to label the cans *A* and *B.*
6. Half fill each can with water. Place the lids on tightly.
7. Hold can *A* with both hands, as shown, and shake it 100 times. The rocks moving in the can are like rocks moving in a stream. Ask another person in the group to shake the can 100 times. Continue passing and shaking the can until it has been shaken 2000 times.
8. Pour the water from can *A* into one of the cups. Observe the water. Put the stones from can *A* back onto the paper towel. Observe the stones.
9. Repeat steps 7 and 8, using the stones in can *B,* but only shake the can 1000 times.
10. Compare the 3 piles of stones.

**Think About It**

1. How are the stones in *A, B,* and *C* different from each other?
2. Why does the water in can *A* look different than that in can *B*?
3. **Challenge** What would happen to the stones in *A* if you shook them in the can 2000 more times?

123

# 4 How Can People Help Control Erosion?

**reforestation**
(rē′fôr ə stā′shən), the replanting of trees.

The house in the picture was built near the ocean. Waves pounded against the shore, eroding the land. The house collapsed.

Every day, water, wind, and ice erode and shape the surface of the earth. But too much erosion at one time can carry away soil that we need. The actions of people add greatly to soil erosion.

In order to get lumber for buildings, people have to cut down many trees. When the trees are gone, the ground is left uncovered. Rain and wind can erode uncovered land more easily than land covered with trees. If the land is left bare, the soil can be washed or blown away.

To reduce soil erosion, people replant the land with new trees. This replanting is called **reforestation.** The person in the picture is reforesting a hillside. Reforestation also makes certain we will have plenty of trees and lumber for the future.

Erosion can cause damage

Reforesting a hillside

124

Fields are strip cropped and contour plowed

**strip cropping,** planting strips of small plants, such as grass or clover, between strips of larger plants.

**contour** (kon′tǔr) **plowing,** plowing rows that go around a hill instead of straight up and down the hill.

Each year, much valuable soil erodes from farmlands. In order to plant crops, farmers must plow the land and uncover the soil. Bare soil will erode quickly. However, farmers can do many things to control the erosion of the soil.

You may have seen farm fields such as the ones above. Farmers often plant strips of grass or clover between strips of crops. This kind of planting is called **strip cropping.** Small plants, such as grass, absorb and hold water better than the large crops. The absorbed water cannot flow down the field and erode the soil. Also, the roots of grass are close together. They hold the soil in place better than the roots of the crops do.

Also notice that the farmer plowed and planted the fields in rows that go around the hill. This kind of plowing is called **contour plowing.** In contour plowing, each row makes a little step—or terrace—around the hill. When it rains, much of the water stays on each terrace and soaks into the land. Suppose the farmer plowed straight up and down the hill. Rainwater would flow quickly down the hill, washing away the soil and seeds.

Have You Heard?
Strip cropping and contour plowing can stop 3/4 of the erosion that occurs on farmlands.

Wind erosion

Trees block wind

## What Are Some Other Ways to Control Erosion?

Find Out

Use a history book or encyclopedia to read about the Dust Bowl of the 1930s.

If sheep and cattle overgraze—or eat too much of the grass—they can cause erosion problems. Without enough grass, the soil in a pasture could be left uncovered. Rain and wind could easily erode the soil and grass roots. A green pasture could be ruined in just a few years! Most ranchers and farmers do not let their livestock overgraze.

Wind erodes dry, bare soil rapidly. You may have seen dust rising from a dry dirt road as a car passes. Strong winds easily erode the dry soil and form a curtain of dust, as shown. To help protect their soil from wind erosion, farmers often plant lines of trees, as shown. The trees block much of the wind that blows across the fields.

### Think About It

1. Define reforestation.
2. How do contour plowing and strip cropping help control erosion?
3. **Challenge** If a field on a hillside is not contour plowed, what do you think might happen to crops at the bottom of the hill?

# Tie It Together

## Sum It Up

Number your paper from 1–10. Complete each sentence by writing the correct word from the list of scrambled words below on your paper. The first and last letter of each word is in the correct place.

RSUT
WNEAHTREIG
TERES
SIOL
CTOOUNR
WTAER
FSROT
BRAE
GCIELAR
SRIPTS

1. The breaking down of rock is called ▦ .

2. ▦ action weathers rocks.

3. Oxygen combines with iron to make ▦ .

4. Weathered rock and decayed organisms are parts of ▦ .

5. Sand in moving ▦ erodes rough stones into smooth pebbles.

6. A ▦ can erode a valley into a U shape.

7. ▦ soil erodes more quickly than a grassy field.

8. ▦ plowing makes small steps that catch rain.

9. To help control erosion, farmers plant crops in ▦ .

10. Lines of ▦ help protect fields from wind erosion.

## Challenge!

1. What do you think causes some soils to be colored red?

2. What do you think would cause more erosion: a stream with sandy water or one with clear water? Why?

3. List three ways that people cause erosion.

4. Suppose you owned land on a hillside that was a field of uncovered soil. What would you do to help control erosion of your land?

## Science Words

carbon dioxide

contour plowing

erosion

frost action

glacier

mineral

oxygen

reforestation

soil

strip cropping

weathering

# Chapter 8
# Our Changing Earth

Pioneers traveling west moved over many different types of land. They crossed wide plains, passed through narrow valleys, and climbed rugged mountains. Over the past two hundred years, cities and towns have changed much of the land. However, the mountains in the picture have not changed much since the pioneers first crossed them. Does that mean they have *always* looked the same? Will the mountains ever look different than they do now?

The lessons in this chapter describe some of the different shapes of the land you see. Some of the land was shaped long ago by huge sheets of ice.

# 1 Predicting Changes

As you grow, your body slowly changes. You may look about the same tomorrow as you do today. But a year from now, you may look different.

The land around us also changes slowly. After millions of years, a high, rocky mountain can change into a low, grassy hill.

Scientists observe the earth today and infer how it looked long ago. They try to predict how the earth will look in the future. The picture shows Niagara Falls. Scientists can measure how fast the falls are eroding the cliffs. The arrow in the drawing shows where scientists think the falls were thousands of years ago.

Try to predict how something around you will change as time passes. Choose an object or a place, such as a house or a vacant lot. Then, draw five pictures of the object or place to show how it might change. Cut out the pictures and mix them up. Ask a classmate to put them in order.

## Think About It

1. How are the first and last pictures different?
2. **Challenge** What do you think will happen to Niagara Falls in the future?

## Have You Heard?

Niagara Falls have been moving up the river at the rate of over 1 meter per year.

Niagara Falls

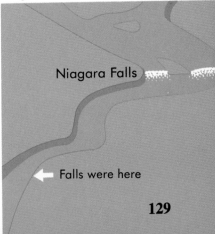

Niagara Falls are moving

Niagara Falls

← Falls were here

# 2 How Did Ice Change the Land?

Sometimes a scientist has to be a clever detective. Like a detective, a scientist often studies clues to explain a mystery.

The pictures show two mysteries that puzzled people for years. Notice the boulders in the field. How did they get there? They did not roll down from a mountain. No mountain is nearby. They are too heavy to be moved by a stream or the wind.

The rock with the large scratches is in New York City's Central Park. What could have cut the straight lines in the rock? People found strange boulders and many scratched rocks like these throughout Europe and North America.

In the meantime, a group of scientists began studying glaciers in the valleys of the Alps Mountains. They noticed large boulders left on the ground where the ice melted years before. The scientists also found many scratches on the rocky surface touched by the glacier. They decided the glaciers had moved the boulders and scratched the surface. The mysteries were solved.

Boulders in field

Scratched rock

Today, scientists think they have solved other mysteries. Most scientists think there have been a number of **ice ages.** An ice age is a time when much of the earth is covered by glaciers—or ice.

During an ice age, the climate of the earth became cooler. Much of the snow that fell in winter did not melt. Year after year the snow built up, forming huge sheets of ice, like the one in the picture. These ice sheets moved slowly over the land. In some places the ice was three kilometers thick. The last ice age began about one million years ago. The map shows how much of the earth was covered by ice.

As the ice sheets moved, they dug up the ground and scraped the sides of hills and mountains. Boulders, pebbles, and soil moved along with the ice. Rocks at the bottom of the moving ice were like claws that scratched the rocky surface of the earth. When the ice melted, rocks and other materials dropped to the ground. Mounds or hills built up.

**ice age,** a long period of time when much of the earth is covered by ice.

## Have You Heard?

If a glacier or ice sheet moves into the ocean, huge blocks of ice break off. These blocks of ice are icebergs that float away in the sea.

Ice sheet

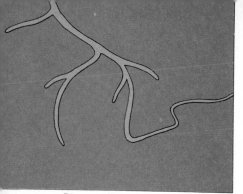

River valleys

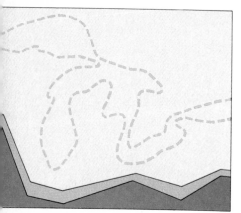

Ice covering valleys

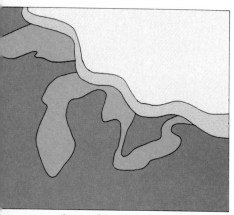

Ice melting

## How Did Ice Form the Great Lakes?

The grinding action of the moving ice left many shallow holes and valleys across the land. These places filled with water and are now small lakes, such as those shown. But the ice also formed five of the largest lakes in the world—the Great Lakes. The drawings explain how scientists think these lakes formed.

The Great Lakes were large river valleys before the last ice age. When the ice sheets came, they eroded the valleys, making them wider and deeper. About fifteen thousand years ago, the ice started melting. Water from the melting ice filled the valleys to form the Great Lakes.

### Think About It

1. What is an ice age?
2. How did the Great Lakes form?
3. **Challenge** Do you think lakes in Texas were formed the same way as lakes in Minnesota? Explain.

Lakes formed by ice

# Discover!

## Camels in Alaska

How would you like to search for camels in Alaska? You may not think of Alaska as the best place to look for camels. You would not find any alive there today, except in zoos. But people have discovered bones that show camels, zebras, and elephants once roamed the Alaskan countryside.

Thousands of years ago, during the last ice age, much of the earth was covered by glaciers. Most of the glaciers' ice came from ocean water. The sea level dropped. The dropping of the sea level uncovered much of the land that is now under water. Scientists think land was uncovered where the Bering Strait is now.

The map shows that the Bering Strait is a narrow strip of water between Asia and North America. But during the last ice age, the land beneath the water was uncovered. Animals could walk from Asia to North America! Many animals found comfortable homes in Alaska and other parts of North America. Mountains provided shelter from the cold weather of the ice age.

After the last ice age, many animals became extinct—or died out. The saber-toothed cat, shown in the drawing, is extinct. This cat was the size of a lion and roamed the forests and fields of North America. The other drawing shows the woolly mammoth, an extinct animal similar to the elephants of today.

While some animals became extinct, others migrated across the land of the Bering Strait. Heading west were camels, zebras, and horses. Coming east were elk, bison, and mountain goats. When the glaciers melted, the sea level rose and cut off the path between the continents.

New discoveries will teach us more about these ice-age wanderers.

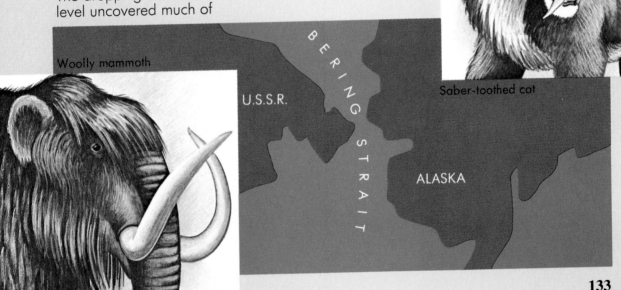

Woolly mammoth

Saber-toothed cat

U.S.S.R.

BERING STRAIT

ALASKA

# 3 How Is the Land Shaped Today?

**landform,** a feature, such as a plain, plateau, hill, or mountain, that gives the land its shape.

**plain** (plān), large area of flat, level land.

**plateau** (pla tō′), large area of level land, but higher than a plain.

Grand Canyon

Imagine taking a trip across the United States. You might meet a lot of interesting people and see many famous sights. You would also notice the different shapes of the land.

The children have made a sand model of the major shapes of the land—or **landforms.** As you read about landforms, compare them to the sand model.

**Plains** are mainly flat and level. They are often found along coasts. But the largest plains in the United States—the Great Plains—are in the middle of the country. This area used to be covered by a large sea. Today, farmers use this fertile land to grow food for people all over the world.

**Plateaus** are higher than plains, but still flat. Plateaus often have rivers that carve out steep valleys—or canyons. A winding river on the Colorado Plateau has cut the Grand Canyon, shown here. Notice that the top of the plateau is flat. Try to imagine how the Colorado Plateau looked before the river carved the canyon.

Mountains and hills are two other major landforms. In North America the tallest and most rugged mountains are in the West. The Appalachian Mountains in the East are more rounded and not as high. Many mountains in a line or in a row are a **mountain range.** Look at the picture of the Teton Range in Wyoming. Each peak is a mountain, but the whole line of peaks is a mountain range.

A mountain less than 300 meters high is often called a hill. Many of the Appalachian Mountains are really hills. The Appalachian Mountains were tall and rugged millions of years ago. Through the years, water and ice eroded the mountains into the low, rolling hills shown.

**mountain range** (rānj), group of mountains in a line.

## Think About It

1. List four major landforms, and give an example of each.
2. **Challenge** Explain how a tall, jagged mountain can become a plain, given enough time.

Appalachian Mountains

Teton Range

# Activity

## Changing Landforms

### Purpose
To change the shape of a landform, using ice.

### You Will Need
- sheet of cardboard
- salt clay
- ice cube with sand
- paper clip or pencil

### Directions
1. Use the salt clay to make a model of a mountain on the sheet of cardboard. Make 3 river valleys, using a paper clip or pencil as shown.
2. Ask your teacher for an ice cube. The ice represents a glacier. Notice the sand on the bottom of the ice cube. What do you think this sand represents?
3. Starting at the top of one of the valleys, press the ice cube—or glacier—down the valley, as shown. Repeat this step for 2 minutes. Notice what happens to the valley.
4. Using the same ice cube, repeat step 3 for the other 2 river valleys.
5. Rest the ice cube on a slant in one of the valleys. Notice what happens when the ice melts.

### Think About It
1. What did the sand in the ice cube represent?
2. What happened to the river valleys as you moved the ice?
3. What happened to the sand in step 5?
4. **Challenge** Describe some ways glaciers can change the shape of a mountain.

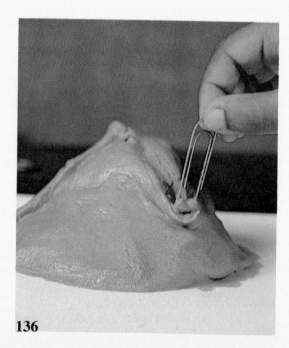
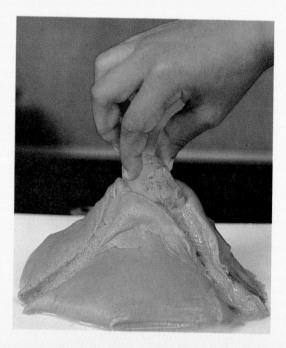

# Tie It Together

## Sum It Up

1. Pretend you are a rock near the bottom of a huge ice sheet. Write a short story describing your journey as the ice sheet moves across the land. Also, describe what happens to you as the ice around you melts.

2. Letter your paper from a–d. From the list below, match each word with the drawing of the landform. Write the name of the landform after the letter it represents.

   plateau     plain
   mountain   hill

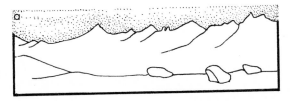

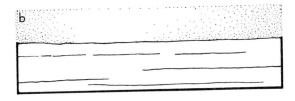

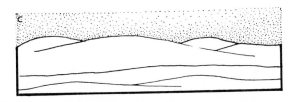

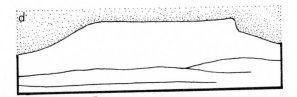

## Challenge!

1. Suppose you found long scratches on rocks in a large area of Vermont. The scratches all point from northwest to southeast and were caused by an ice sheet. From what direction did the ice sheet probably come? Explain your answer.

2. Imagine you are a pioneer traveling west. Describe the landforms you would see in the West that you might not see in the East.

3. Plateaus are often called tablelands. How do you think they got this name?

4. Explain how a plateau with many rivers can look like a small mountain range.

## Science Words

ice age

landform

mountain range

plain

plateau

# Laboratory

## Erosion by Water

*a*

### Purpose
To compare how clear water and water with rock and soil particles erode solid materials.

### You Will Need
- spoon
- fine sand
- 2 plastic margarine tubs with lids
- water-soluble glue
- centimeter ruler
- balance
- water
- 5 small rocks

### Stating the Problem
Suppose a house is built on a cliff that overlooks a fast-moving river. The moving water might erode the ground under the house. Will the river erode the ground faster if the river carries a lot of rock and soil particles or fewer of such particles? What do you predict?

### Investigating the Problem
1. Place about 8 spoonfuls of sand in one of the plastic tubs. Stir in enough glue to make a stiff mixture, as shown in picture *a*. Divide the mixture into 2 equal parts.
2. Shape 2 cubes with the mixture. Each cube should be about 3 cm on each side, as shown in picture *b*. Put the cubes where they can harden overnight. Wash out the tubs.
3. Measure and record the weight of each hardened cube, as shown in picture *c*.
4. Half fill each tub with water. Add 5 small rocks to one of the plastic tubs. Place 1 cube in each tub. Tightly cover each tub, and shake it 50 times.
5. Take out the rocks. Compare the contents of the tubs. Measure and record the weight of each cube.

b

## Making Conclusions

1. Explain any differences that you observed between the 2 cubes in step 5.
2. Why did you measure the weights of the cubes before shaking them?
3. Was your prediction about the cliff under the house correct? Explain.
4. How could you make the water in the plastic tub erode more of the cube?

c

# Careers

### Agronomist

"Something is wrong with my fruit trees!" My garden is overrun with insects."

These are just some kinds of problems that people have when they call me up," says Karen, who is an agronomist. An agronomist is interested in soil and the nutrients needed to grow plants. Karen also helps farmers control erosion.

"Sometimes I get thirty calls a day. Most of the questions are about insects. People want to identify and control insects that are eating their plants.

"Sometimes peoples' plants do not grow well because of the soil. I tell them to take a sample of their soil and to bring it to my office. When I get the soil sample, I send it to the lab. We analyze

about one thousand soil samples a year. In the lab we can find out what kinds of chemicals are in the soil. Then, I can tell people what kind of fertilizers to put on their gardens to help the plants grow."

Karen's interest in soil and plants began when she was a girl growing up on a farm. Karen wanted to learn as much as she could about the soil so she could help farmers and gardeners. In college she studied agricultural science.

Today, many farmers in the county seek Karen's advice about soil erosion and growing crops. But only about five hundred farms are left in her county. So Karen usually advises people interested in gardens.

Besides talking to individual farmers and gardeners, Karen talks to groups at the university, libraries, and parks. "My favorite part of this job is helping so many people understand the problems in their fields or gardens. Then, I can suggest ways in which they can correct the problems themselves."

Cartographer

Surveyor

The shape of the earth's surface affects where and how we live. People in some careers spend a lot of time working with the earth's surface.

Perhaps the greatest number of people who work with the earth's surface are **farmers.** North American farmers grow food for people all around the world.

Scientists often work with farmers to choose farming methods that will add nutrients to the soil. Farmers also try to guard against soil erosion.

**Landscapers** also work with the land. The beautiful shrubs and lawns around office buildings are the work of landscapers. Many homeowners hire landscapers to plant sod and shrubs around their houses. The beautiful work of landscapers can also be seen along our nation's highways.

People wanting to be farmers and landscapers should have a high-school education.

Before going on a trip, you or your parents may look at a map. Most maps begin as photographs. **Aerial photographers** use special cameras to photograph large areas of land from airplanes. **Cartographers**—or map makers—use these photographs to make maps. They use special instruments to draw the maps.

Much of the information that cartographers use comes from **surveyors.** These people measure exact distances and elevations on the earth's surface. The property boundaries of your house or apartment building were measured by a surveyor. A surveyor also makes measurements for the builders of roads and other structures.

Cartographers and surveyors have gone to college. Photographers usually go to schools of photography after high school.

# On Your Own

## Picture Clue

The picture on the first page of this unit might remind you of a duck or a dog. You know that the wind sometimes blows clouds into shapes of animals. The picture shows that wind can be a good sculptor too.

## Projects

1. Use an encyclopedia or library book to find out which parts of the United States were under ice during the last ice age. On a large map, carefully draw a line showing how far south the ice came in the United States.

2. Collect pictures from magazines showing the four major landforms. Arrange the pictures in a scrapbook. Be sure to write, beneath each picture, where the landform is located.

3. Observe a river. Take several pictures which show how the river erodes the land. Tape the pictures on posterboard and write a description of each picture.

## Books About Science

*The Earth and Its Wonders* by John Thackray. Larousse, 1980. The world is full of natural wonders. Become aware of the movement and excitement of the earth around you.

*Glaciers, Nature's Frozen Rivers* by Hershell and Joan Nixen. Dodd Mead, 1980. Learn more about glaciers and how they move. How can we put glaciers to use for people?

*A Spit Is a Piece of Land* by Doris Coburn. Messner, 1978. Learn more about the landforms shaped by forces inside the earth and on the earth's surface.

# Unit Test

## Multiple Choice

Number your paper from 1–5. Next to each number, write the letter of the word or words that best complete the statement or answer the question.

1. Weathering is
   a. the movement of rocks.
   b. the growth of plants.
   c. rain, wind, and temperature.
   d. the breaking down of rock.

2. Erosion is
   a. the building of mountains.
   b. the wearing away and movement of materials by water, wind, and ice.
   c. a collection of rocks at the bottom of a hill.
   d. caused only by rivers.

3. People can help control erosion by
   a. reforesting.
   b. contour plowing.
   c. strip cropping.
   d. Answers a, b, and c are correct.

4. The Grand Canyon is cut into a
   a. plain.
   b. plateau.
   c. mountain.
   d. hill.

5. Rocks are made of
   a. carbon dioxide.
   b. oxygen.
   c. soil.
   d. minerals.

## True or False

Number your paper from 6–10. Next to each number, write *true* if the sentence is correct and *false* if the sentence is incorrect. Make each false statement true by changing the underlined word or words and writing the correct word or words on your paper.

6. Frost action is the breaking apart of rocks and causes weathering.

7. Scratched rocks and boulders in open fields are clues that glaciers covered an area.

8. The Great Lakes were formed by dams.

9. A jagged piece of rock in a stream will stay jagged.

10. Bare soil erodes more slowly than soil covered with grass.

# UNIT FIVE
# ADAPTATIONS TO SURROUNDINGS

Chapter 9  Adaptations to Climate

Chapter 10  Adaptations to Water

Little friend in a
  saguaro
Hooting through the
  night.
But as morning comes
He sleeps in the
  heart of his home.

Kristian Montana *age 10*

# Chapter 9
# Adaptations to Climate

Living things are found on every part of the earth. Penguins live in cold, snowy places. The penguins in the picture can dive into the sea to hunt for food. They can swim for long periods of time in the icy water.

The lessons in this chapter describe how organisms can live in different climates. You will learn why some organisms look the way they do.

1 Observing Plants That Store Water

2 How Are Organisms Adapted to the Desert?

3 How Are Organisms Adapted to Cold Places?

4 How Are Organisms Adapted to Seasonal Changes?

# 1 Observing Plants That Store Water

Most living things need food, air, water, and space. In some places water is scarce. If you hike in a desert, you can carry a water supply. But how do plants in dry places get water?

Even dry places get a little rain and dew. Some plants store rainwater in thick leaves or stems. They use the stored water during dry times.

Hold a leaf from a plant that has thick leaves like those on the jade plant in the picture. Cut the leaf in half. Look at the inside of the leaf with a hand lens. Squeeze your leaf, and feel the moisture.

The cactus plant has a thick stem. Compare the picture of the inside of a cactus stem with the inside of your leaf.

## Think About It

1. How does the inside of your leaf look like the inside of a cactus stem?
2. How could storing water help a desert plant?
3. **Challenge** Could a plant with thick leaves live without any rainfall? Explain your answer.

Jade plant leaf

Cactus

# 2 How Are Organisms Adapted to the Desert?

**adapt** (ə dapt′), make fit to live under certain conditions.

**organism** (ôr′gə niz′əm), a living thing.

Cactus

The dry, sandy desert in the picture gets little rain. In the daytime, moisture sinks into the sand or evaporates into the hot, dry air. The temperature can be higher than 40°Celsius during the day. But at night deserts cool quickly. The temperature can drop to 0°Celsius, cold enough to freeze water. You might not find a desert a very comfortable place to live. But many living things—or **organisms**—are found in the desert.

When it rains, cactus plants in the desert take in water through their shallow roots. They store the water in their thick stems. During dry times cactus plants use the stored water. Because they can store water, cactus plants can live in the desert. They are fitted—or **adapted**—to life in the desert.

Other plants are adapted to desert life. Some have waxy coatings on their leaves. The waxy coatings help keep moisture inside the leaves. Some desert plants bloom only after heavy rains. The plants die during dry times, but their seeds remain alive in the ground. When the rains come, the seeds sprout and grow into plants. The plants bloom and produce more seeds. A four-o'clock plant that grows in the desert in North Africa can sprout, bloom, and produce seeds in about a week.

Desert animals, such as some lizards, snakes, birds, spiders, and scorpions, are adapted to the desert's heat and dryness. During the day these animals avoid the sun's heat by staying under the ground or in the shade. At night they come out to hunt for food. At dawn they return to their shelters.

Drinking water is scarce in the desert. Most desert animals get water from the food they eat. Many small animals, such as the desert wood rat, get water by eating the juicy leaves, stems, and roots of plants. Larger animals, such as the kit fox, get some of their water from the bodies of small animals that they eat.

The kangaroo rat in the picture does not need to drink water. Its body loses very little water. The kangaroo rat can make the water it needs from the food it eats. This ability is an **adaptation** that helps the kangaroo rat survive.

## Think About It

1. List two ways that plants adapt to the desert.
2. List two ways that animals adapt to the desert.
3. **Challenge** When is the best time to observe animals in the desert? Why do you think so?

Kangaroo rat

Find Out
    Use the library to find out how camels can travel in the desert for a week without water and up to 10 days without food.

**adaptation** (ad′ap tā′shən), a structure, form, or habit that helps an organism live in its surroundings.

# 3 How Are Organisms Adapted to Cold Places?

tundra (tun′drə), a vast, cold, treeless region in northern North America, Europe, and Asia, and on high mountains.

Many people live in places where it is cold and snowy for part of each year. They wear heavy clothes to protect themselves from the cold. Parts of the earth are covered with ice and snow almost all year. Some organisms are adapted to the cold.

Large parts of northern North America, Europe, and Asia have a cold, dry climate. The temperature stays above freezing all day for only a few weeks of the year. Other times, it drops as low as −50° Celsius. Strong, cold winds blow almost all the time. In these places, called the **tundra,** the ground is frozen almost all year. Tundra is also found on high mountains.

During the few warm weeks the top inches of frozen soil thaw. Seeds in the soil sprout. Young plants push roots into the ground and grow. Most plants on the tundra have small leaves and roots. They grow in clumps close to the ground. There they are protected from freezing winds. Notice the tiny hairs on the stems and leaves of these plants. They help keep the plant warm. The hairs trap air and keep the wind from drying the plant.

Tiny hairs help keep plants warm

150

Walrus

Animals on the tundra also are adapted to cold and snow. Fat and fur help mammals keep their bodies at the same temperature all the time. The walrus in the picture has a layer of fat about 8 centimeters thick beneath its tough skin. Thick, oily fur keeps the polar bear warm. The fur traps a layer of air that keeps the bear's body heat inside. Fat and fur protect these animals from the icy waters in which they hunt food.

Penguins live in cold places near the South Pole. Closely packed, scalelike feathers help keep the bird's body heat inside. Like mammals, birds' temperatures are controlled within their bodies. Feathers trap warm air next to the bird's skin.

## Think About It

1. List two ways in which plants are adapted to life on the tundra.
2. How do fat, fur, and feathers help animals that live in cold places?
3. **Challenge** If an animal that could not keep its temperature the same all the time went to the tundra, what might happen to it?

### Have You Heard?

The polar bear's whitish fur makes the bear hard to see against the snow and ice. The soles of a polar bear's feet are covered with thick fur. This fur keeps the polar bear from slipping when it moves about on the ice.

# 4 How Are Organisms Adapted to Seasonal Changes?

Many places have four distinct seasons each year—spring, summer, fall, and winter. Days are longest in summer, shorter in fall, and shortest in winter. Days grow longer again in spring.

Some plants are adapted to seasonal changes. An **annual** is a plant, such as a marigold, that produces flowers and seeds in the warm seasons of one year. The plant dies, but its seeds stay alive throughout the winter. In spring the seeds sprout, and new plants grow. A **perennial** can stay alive for many years. The same plant produces flowers and seeds each year. Plant parts above the ground may die in winter. Roots stay alive beneath the soil where they are protected from cold. Grasses and tulips are perennials.

Trees and bushes also stay alive during winter. Trees with broad leaves, such as this apple tree, produce new shoots and flowers in spring. Leaves and stems grow during summer. Toward fall, seeds that will form new plants develop inside the fruit. Later, leaves and fruit fall from the tree. Seeds stay in the ground through the winter. In spring, some seeds sprout and begin to grow into new trees.

**annual** (an′yü əl), plant that lives only 1 year.

**perennial** (pə ren′ē əl), plant that can live 2 years or more.

Spring

Summer

You may have noticed that a pet dog has a thicker coat in winter than it does in summer. When summer comes, the dog sheds some of its hair. The heavy winter coat thins out. In fall, the dog's coat grows thicker again.

Many animals grow thicker fur or longer feathers as winter comes. The fur keeps the animal's body heat inside in cold weather. In summer, the heavy winter coat thins out, and the animal does not get too warm in hot weather.

The weasel is active outdoors all year. Its fur changes color with the seasons. In late fall, white hairs begin to appear in the weasel's coat. By winter, the weasel has a white coat. Look at the picture of the weasel in winter. Notice that the white coat is hard to see against the snow. In spring, dark hairs begin to appear in the weasel's white coat. The weasel's coat is brown in summer and fall. Look at the picture of the weasel in summer and fall. Notice that the brown fur is harder to see against the ground. If the weasel did not have this adaptation for changes in the seasons, it would be easy for enemies to see.

Winter

Summer and fall

## How Do the Seasons Affect Animal Behavior?

Have You Heard?
In winter, frogs bury themselves in the mud at the bottom of shallow ponds. In spring the frog digs its way out of the mud.

**hibernate** (hī′bər nāt), spend the winter in a state in which all the functions of the body slow down greatly.

**migrate** (mī′grāt), go from one region to another with the changes in seasons.

Many animals live in underground dens in winter. Field mice gather extra food in fall and store it in their dens. They eat the stored food in winter. Bears eat extra food in fall. They store the food as layers of fat in their bodies. In winter, bears sleep in their dens. They live on stored fat. Woodchucks also eat extra food in fall and store it as fat. They **hibernate** all winter. The woodchuck in the picture is hibernating and is using little energy. It lives on stored body fat. When an animal hibernates, the temperature of its body drops greatly. The animal appears to be in a very deep sleep.

Some animals go to different places—or **migrate**—when the seasons change. Flocks of geese fly to warmer places in the late fall. In spring they fly to places that have cooler weather.

### Think About It

1. List two ways in which plants are adapted to changing seasons.
2. List two ways in which animals are adapted to changing seasons.
3. **Challenge** What might happen to a woodchuck that did not eat extra food in the fall?

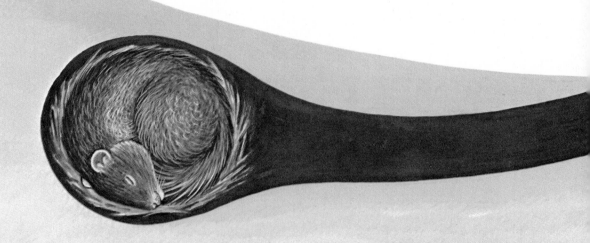

# Do You Know?

## Foxes Adapt to Climates

Arctic fox

The sunlight beats down upon the land as another day slowly passes in a western American desert. A warm breeze gently bends a patch of colorful wildflowers on a sandy hill. In a den beneath the hill, a kit fox lies sleeping.

Three thousand kilometers away, a fresh blanket of snow covers the Canadian tundra. The only sounds to be heard are the crunch crunch crunch of a polar bear stomping through the snow. Behind the bear, at a safe distance, is the white figure of an arctic fox.

The desert and tundra have very different climates. Yet, foxes survive in both places. As with other organisms, the secret to survival is adaptation. The pictures show some ways the kit fox and the arctic fox have adapted to their climates.

One important adaptation is color. Like

Kit fox

many other arctic animals, the arctic fox has white fur in winter that lets it blend into its surroundings. During the short summer its fur turns to shades of brown.

A white fox in the desert might not survive very well. Its light color would make it an easy target for coyotes.

Look at the pictures of the foxes again. Besides color, something else is different between these two animals. The kit fox has long, pointed ears. The arctic fox has short, stubby ears.

In order for a kit fox to survive in the desert, the

fox must get rid of much of its body heat. A lot of the fox's body heat escapes through its ears. Large ears allow more heat to escape, so the fox stays cooler.

How do you think the arctic fox's ears help it survive? These small ears keep in as much of the fox's body heat as possible. Its heavy fur coat and bushy tail also help keep the arctic fox warm.

When you see pictures of wild animals, study the animals closely. See if you can pick out certain ways the animals have adapted to their surroundings.

# Activity

## Inferring Adaptations

**Purpose**
To infer what adaptations an animal that migrates from the tundra to the desert might have.

**You Will Need**
- drawing paper
- crayons or colored pencils
- colored paper
- scraps of cloth
- clay or pieces of wood
- glue or tape

**Directions**
1. Cold, windy tundra areas are found high on the tops of some mountains. A desert might lie at the base of the mountain, as shown. Imagine an animal that migrates each year from the desert to the tundra.
2. From what you know about adaptations, infer what adaptations your animal needs to survive in these 2 places.
3. Draw or build a model of your animal.
4. Tell how your animal gets enough food and water. Describe where it lives.
5. Tell what adaptations help your animal stay comfortable at different temperatures.
6. Tell how your animal protects itself from other animals.

**Think About It**
1. Which adaptation is most important in helping your animal survive in the desert?
2. How does your animal's behavior change when it migrates from the tundra to the desert?
3. **Challenge** In which place does your imaginary animal raise its young? Explain your choice.

156

# Tie It Together

## Sum It Up

On a piece of paper, write the numbers 1 to 4. Next to numbers 1, 2, and 3, draw a plant or an animal that could live in each of the three following climates: 1) hot and dry, 2) cold and windy, and 3) changing seasons. Below its picture, write a sentence about each organism you drew. Describe an adaptation that helps the organism stay alive. Next to number 4, draw a picture of a hibernating animal.

## Challenge!

1. In what ways are the adaptations needed by desert and tundra animals alike?

2. How do feathers help a bird that migrates from warm to cold climates?

3. How is the means of keeping warm similar in tundra plants and animals?

4. How do migrating and hibernating help animals survive?

5. What kinds of places are most difficult for animals to live in? For plants to live in? Why do you think so?

## Science Words

adapt

adaptation

annual

hibernate

migrate

organism

perennial

tundra

# Chapter 10
# Adaptations to Water

If you walk along a beach like the one in the picture, you might not see any familiar plants or animals. Look closely into the shallow water. Notice the seaweed in the water. Many kinds of organisms are adapted to living in or near the oceans, lakes, streams, ponds, and marshy places on the earth.

The lessons in this chapter describe how organisms have adapted to life in different kinds of water. You will learn why most fish in river water cannot survive in ocean water.

1 Imagining Life in the Water

2 How Are Organisms Adapted to Life in Fresh Water?

3 How Are Organisms Adapted to Life in Wetlands?

4 How Are Organisms Adapted to Life in the Oceans?

# 1 Imagining Life in the Water

Many people like to swim and play in water. But people cannot live in the water as fish do. People cannot get oxygen, find food, or move about underwater for long periods of time. Fish are adapted to life in the water.

Think about a beach or a shallow pond like the one in the picture. Design a plant or animal that could live in or near the water. Draw or make a model of your plant or animal. You might design a bird that eats fish. You might make a plant that grows on the ocean bottom. Show how the plant would get sunshine and water. Show how the animal would move, get oxygen, and find food.

## Think About It

1. What adaptations does your plant or animal have for living in or near water?
2. **Challenge** What kinds of new adaptations would people need to live underwater?

Many organisms in shallow pool

# 2 How Are Organisms Adapted to Life in Fresh Water?

Almost every city or town has a lake, pond, or stream nearby. Maybe you have waded into a muddy pond to look for tadpoles. You might have walked along a stream, looking for minnows. If so, you know that many kinds of plants and animals live in freshwater lakes, ponds, and streams.

Many plants that live in lakes and ponds have long stems. The water lilies in the picture live in the quiet water of a pond. Their roots grow in the bottom of the pond. Their long, thin stems stretch up toward the surface of the water. Their flowers and large, flat leaves float on top of the water.

The carpet moss is different from the water lilies. Carpet moss lives where water moves quickly in a stream. The moss clings tightly to the rock, so the moss is not moved along with the current.

Carpet moss

Water lilies

160

When you think about animals that live in fresh water, you probably think of fish. The body of the fish slips easily through the water. Fins and a tail help the fish stop, turn, and move. A fish cannot breathe in air as you do. Instead, fish have **gills** that take in oxygen from water. A covering on the side of the fish's head protects the gills. As the fish moves, water flows into its mouth. The drawing shows how water moves across the gills and out.

Some fish have protective coloring. The fish shown here has light-colored scales on its belly. To an enemy below, the fish seems to blend with the sky. The fish has darker scales on its back. To an enemy from above, the fish looks like part of the bottom of the lake or stream.

**gills** (gilz), parts of a water animal's body through which the animal takes oxygen from water and gives off carbon dioxide.

Water moves across the gills

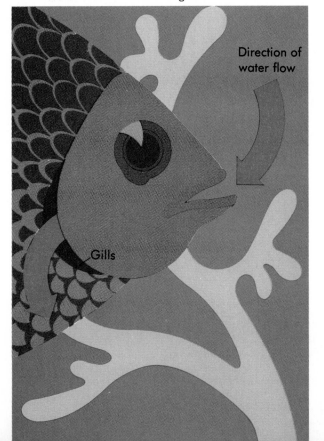

Direction of water flow

Gills

Color protects fish

## What Animals Live Part of Their Lives in Fresh Water?

Some animals that breathe air live part of their lives in the water. The adult mayfly can fly in the air. A young mayfly looks somewhat like the adult. But it has gills and lives in the water. Notice this young mayfly's strong claws. These claws help it cling to rocks. Its curved body hugs the rock and keeps the mayfly from being washed away.

Tadpoles have gills and live in the water. Adult frogs, however, have lungs and breathe air. They live in moist places along the shore. Frogs swim among the plants in shallow water. They use their long, sticky tongues to catch insects.

### Find Out
The water boatman gets its name from the legs it uses like oars. Use an encyclopedia or reference book to find out what other special features help the water boatman live in freshwater ponds and streams.

## Think About It

1. List three ways in which animals are adapted to life in fresh water.
2. How is a water lily adapted to life in quiet ponds?
3. **Challenge** Could a water lily live in the middle of a fast-moving stream? Explain your answer.

Young mayfly

# Do You Know?

## Fish Make Electricity

It was another warm, muggy day around the Amazon River in South America. A horse was bending down to take a drink from the water. Suddenly, the horse jolted backward, falling to the ground. This animal had just had an unfriendly meeting with an electric eel!

An electric eel, such as the one shown, lives in many freshwater rivers of South America. This unusual fish makes electricity in its body. This eel has organs that work like batteries.

The electricity it makes surrounds its body, forming an electric field. The eel uses this electric field as protection against enemies and for capturing food.

Anything that gets too close to the eel crosses the electric field. The eel then knows something is within range of getting shocked. The electric eel

Electric eel

does not even have to touch its victim to kill it. This amazing animal sends out electric shocks that stun or kill small fish. The closer an organism is to the eel, the stronger the shock can be.

The shock is only strong enough to kill small animals, such as frogs and fish. But larger animals, such as horses and humans, have been thrown off their feet when they accidentally stepped on an electric eel.

The eel's electricity has another important use. The eel lives in rivers that are often dark and muddy. It could be difficult for a fish to see

where it is going. To make matters worse, an electric eel loses its eyesight as it grows into an adult. How does the eel move about without bumping things? The eel has adapted to its surroundings by using its electricity to "see." As the eel swims, objects, such as rocks, may cross the electric field. The eel then knows where the rocks are and can avoid hitting them.

Every living thing has special ways of adapting to its surroundings. The electric eel's "sixth sense" of electricity has allowed it to adapt and survive in its freshwater home.

# 3 How Are Organisms Adapted to Life in Wetlands?

**wetland,** place where water collects on land.

Mud puddles often stay on the ground after a heavy rain. Later, the water evaporates or sinks into the soil. In a **wetland** the ground has so much water, it is wet most of the year. Marshes and swamps are kinds of wetlands.

Some wetlands have water a meter or more deep. In others the land is almost like a wet sponge. At one time people thought these wet, soggy places were useless. Many wetlands were drained and filled in to make room for farms and buildings. Today, scientists know wetlands are important. These places soak up and hold water. Many organisms spend at least part of their lives in wetlands.

Some wetlands were once lakes or ponds. Plants and soil filled in the lakes and ponds. The ground is covered with water some parts of the year. Certain trees and bushes grow well in the wet soil. Notice how these cranberry bushes form a thick mat over the water.

Many animals are adapted to living in wetlands. Ducks and geese eat seeds, young plants, insects, and small fish found in wetlands. The gray, black, brown, and green colors of the ducks' feathers help protect them. The colors blend with the earth and plants around them. Many animals hide their nests in the tall grasses.

Cranberry bushes

Heron wading

The marsh rice rat lives in the wetlands. It weaves a nest of grass. On very wet ground the rat hangs its nest on a tall stem. In dryer places the rat hides the nest under a log. This rat swims in shallow water to catch small fish and snails. The rat can also hunt food on land. The marsh rice rat is food for other animals, such as hawks, owls, and snakes, that live in or near wetlands.

The wetland in the picture is the Everglades in Florida. Tall palms, cypress trees, and many kinds of grasses grow here. Alligators, frogs, turtles, and birds live in the Everglades. Notice how this heron is adapted to the wetland. A heron wades in shallow water on long legs. It spears fish with its long bill.

## Have You Heard?

A salt marsh can form where the ocean meets the land. The young of many ocean fish live in salt marshes. Decayed material makes the soil in a salt marsh very rich.

## Think About It

1. How is the marsh rice rat adapted to wetlands?
2. How is the heron adapted to wetlands?
3. **Challenge** When wetlands are drained, what do you think happens to organisms that live there?

# 4 How Are Organisms Adapted to Life in the Oceans?

Most of the water on earth is in the oceans. Ocean water has so much salt that a mouthful of ocean water tastes saltier than a mouthful of potato chips. Organisms that live in or near the ocean are adapted to living in this salt water. Most ocean organisms cannot live in fresh water.

Look at the pictures of the rocky shore. The picture on the left shows high tide. Much of the shore is covered with water. The picture on the right shows low tide. Notice the seaweed that stays on the rocks as the water falls with the tide. Seaweed can live in the drying sun and the pounding waves because it is tough and leathery.

During low tide the shore comes alive with animals. Crabs, worms, and snails crawl out to look for food. During high tide they dig themselves under the sand. Shore animals, such as clams, have many adaptations to life near the ocean. The clam's shell blends with its surroundings. Enemies have a harder time finding the animal. The clam opens its shell to eat. Water flows in, carrying tiny organisms. The clam strains them from the water and eats them.

High tide

Low tide

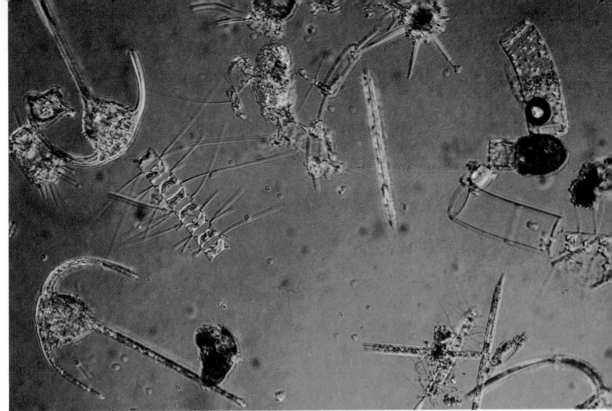
Plankton

If you looked at the ocean's surface, you might think no organisms lived there. The water is deep and cold. Sunlight does not reach the ocean bottom. But many organisms are adapted to life in the open ocean.

Huge groups of tiny organisms called **plankton** float about all over the ocean. In some places, you could find more than twelve million plankton in a bucket of water. Some of the plankton in the picture are like green plants. They can make food from sunlight. Other kinds of plankton are tiny animals and animallike organisms. They eat the plantlike plankton.

Almost every ocean animal depends on plankton in some way. For example, small fish eat plankton. Larger fish or large ocean birds eat the small fish. Clams and other animals near the shore also eat plankton. Many huge whales feed on plankton.

**plankton** (plangk′tən), small organisms that float in water.

**167**

### How Do Organisms Adapt to Life in Deep Water?

Some ocean animals must breathe air. Whales and dolphins are mammals that live their whole lives in the water. They are shaped somewhat like fish. But they do not have gills like fish. They breathe through lungs like those of animals that live on land. Some kinds of whales can hold their breath under water for as long as two hours. Then, they must come to the surface to breathe. The whale in the picture is letting out air from its lungs. It lets air out through an opening on the top of its head. The spout forms when the whale's warm, moist breath meets the cooler air over the ocean. Mist forms, just as your breath forms mist on a cold day. Before the whale dives, it takes in fresh air.

No light reaches the deepest part of the ocean. Most fish of the deep are dark colored. They have large mouths and sharp teeth. This hatchet fish can open its mouth wide enough to swallow a fish its own size.

Huge amounts of water press down on the deep parts of the ocean. Deepwater fish are adapted to living with this high pressure. Most of these fish cannot live near the surface. They would swell up like balloons in the lower pressure at the surface.

## Have You Heard?

Many deepwater fish give off light. A fishing line with a light hanging on the end grows from the head of one kind of fish. Another fish lights up the roof of its mouth. Scientists think the lights help fish attract food or mates.

## Think About It

1. List two ways in which some animals are adapted to changing tides.
2. List two ways animals are adapted to life in the open ocean.
3. **Challenge** What is most difficult about studying organisms that live on the ocean bottom?

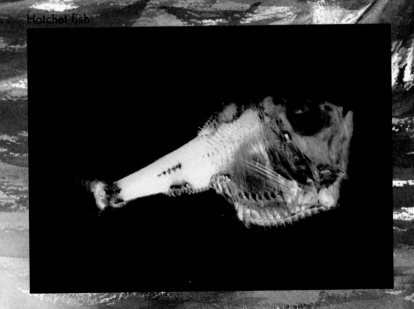
Hatchet fish

169

# Activity

## Observing Plants in Fresh Water and in Seawater

### Purpose
To observe how a plant lives in fresh water and in seawater.

### You Will Need
- gravel
- 2 large jars
- measuring cup
- water
- 50 mL of salt
- spoon
- paper for labels
- marking pen
- 2 water plants of the same kind

### Directions
1. Put a layer of gravel 2 or 3 cm deep in each jar.
2. Using the measuring cup, measure 2 L of tap water into each jar.
3. Pour 50 mL of salt into one of the jars. With your spoon, stir the salt until it dissolves.
4. Label the jar with salt in it *artificial seawater*. Label the other jar *fresh water*. Let the jars stand overnight.
5. Plant the same kind of water plant in the gravel in each jar.
6. Place both jars in a lighted area. Let the plants grow for a week. Add tap water as needed to replace any that evaporates.
7. Observe the plants every day for a week. Each day, record any changes you see in the plants.

### Think About It
1. How did the plants change after a week? Were the 2 plants still alike?
2. Do you think these plants normally live in freshwater lakes and ponds or in the salty oceans? Why do you think so?
3. **Challenge** How could you find out how different amounts of salt will affect a plant?

# Tie It Together

## Sum It Up

1. On a sheet of paper, draw a picture showing three organisms that might live in a pond. Name the organisms in your drawing and label them *a, b,* and *c*. Write the letters *a, b,* and *c* at the bottom of your paper. Next to each letter, write a sentence that tells how that organism is adapted to life in fresh water.

2. The picture below shows a wetlands animal. Write the letter *d* on your paper. Next to the letter, tell what the organism might eat and how it might live.

3. Write the letter *e* on your paper. Next to the letter, draw an ocean animal. Explain how the animal gets oxygen and food.

## Challenge!

1. Where do you think an animal that has both lungs and gills might live?

2. List some adaptations a fish could use to both catch food and defend itself.

3. Could you grow cranberries in a garden? Why or why not?

4. Parts of the ocean where a great many plankton live are often good fishing grounds. Why do you think this is so?

5. In what ways are whales like fish? In what ways are they like land animals?

## Science Words

gills

plankton

wetland

# Laboratory

## Growing Plants Under Different Conditions

*a*

**Purpose**
To compare what happens when 1 kind of plant is grown in forest and in desert conditions.

**You Will Need**
• 2 large, wide-mouthed jars
• coarse gravel
• potting soil
• sand
• woodland plants
• long-handled spoon
• water
• torn leaves
• clear plastic wrap
• rubber band

**Stating the Problem**
Organisms are well suited, or adapted, to different areas on the earth. For example, a plant that lives in a cool, shady forest might have many broad leaves to soak up the sunlight. Suppose the forest dries up and becomes a desert. Will the broad-leaved woodland plant be able to live there? What do you predict might happen to a woodland plant growing in a desert? Write down your prediction.

**Investigating the Problem**
1. With a partner, you will build both a forest and a desert jar. Study pictures *a* and *b*.
2. Clean 2 large jars. Put a layer of gravel, 3 cm deep, in the bottom of each jar.
3. Put a 6-cm layer of potting soil on top of the gravel for the forest jar. Put a 6-cm layer of sand on top of the gravel for the desert jar.
4. Choose a type of woodland plant for your experiment like the plants in the pictures. Place 1 plant in each jar. Use the spoon to gently place the plants in the soil or sand. Then, spoon

more potting soil around the plant in the forest jar. Spoon more sand around the plant in the desert jar. Dampen the soil and sand in each jar. Do not completely wet the soil or sand. Make sure the plants are set firmly in the soil or sand.

5. Sprinkle some leaf pieces around the plant in the forest jar, as shown in picture *a*. Use a piece of plastic wrap to cover the top of the forest jar. The plastic will hold moisture in the forest jar just as the leaves of tall trees hold moisture in a real forest. Place the jar in a sunny spot.

6. Keep your desert jar uncovered. Place it in a sunny spot on a window ledge. Keep both jars away from the heating vents in your classroom.

7. Observe your plants closely for a week. Keep the forest jar moist like the jar in picture *a*. Lightly water the forest jar once during the week to provide the plant with as much water as it might get from rainfall. The desert jar should be kept dry like the jar in picture *b*.

**Making Conclusions**

1. Describe how the 2 plants looked after a week. Was your prediction about what would happen to the woodland plant in the desert correct?

2. How is the woodland plant fit or unfit for the desert conditions? What might help the plant survive in the desert?

3. What might happen if a desert plant were grown in a forest jar?

4. What might happen to a woodland plant if the forest in which it grew became hot like a jungle?

5. Name four changes in conditions that affect the survival of a plant.

*b*

# Careers

## Naturalist

"I like to think of the place where I work as an oasis," says Sandy. "Almost every large city has forest preserves and nature centers nearby. They let people stay in touch with nature."

Sandy is a naturalist at a nature center near a big city.

"Part of my job is to be a guide for our visitors. Over 100,000 people a year come here to walk on our 5 kilometers of hiking trails. I tell them about the three types of areas we have here—forest, prairie, and wetlands. I also give them an idea of some of the plants and animals they may see on the trail."

During the spring and fall, school groups take field trips to the nature center. Sandy reminds the students that it is important to stay on the trails. "I ask the students not to make noise so they do not frighten the racoons, deer, and other animals along the trail."

Sandy remembers spending a lot of time outside with her family. She learned to love nature as she spent more time in forests. "A lot of people think I have a great job because I work outside around plants and animals. I do have a great job. But I did not get the job just because I like wildlife. In college, I studied life science and earth science. I studied and observed nature to learn as much as I could. The visitors appreciate the knowledge I can give them."

Over the last few years, Sandy has noticed people respecting wildlife more and more. "We have almost no problems with people littering the trails. The more our visitors learn about the environment, the better they take care of it."

Zoologist

Marine biologist

Much of the information in this unit is a result of discoveries made by **zoologists.** A zoologist observes and studies animals. They discover how the animals live and where they live. Most zoologists study one kind of animal, such as bears or hawks.

To be a zoologist, you must go to college for at least four years.

A wide variety of jobs deal with animals in the ocean environment.

If you have an interest in sharks, seahorses, and other sea life, you might like to be a **marine biologist.** This scientist explores and studies underwater organisms. A group of marine biologists may take ocean voyages to study sea life.

Marine biologists go to college for four to seven years.

Some biologists study the habits of dolphins and killer whales. People are interested in these animals because they can be well-trained. A **marine animal trainer** works with these animals every day to teach them tricks and skills. The trainer knows the habits of the animal. He or she also knows that a wild animal can be dangerous as well as playful.

You can learn to train marine animals by working on the job with other trainers.

Some people study sea animals. Some people train them. Other people collect sea animals to use for food. A **shellfish harvester** collects clams, oysters, and mussels, which are sold to stores and restaurants. Shellfish harvesters often gather the shellfish at low tide. They can wade out into the water and pick the shellfish up with their hands or with a rake. These workers learn their skills while on the job.

# On Your Own

## Picture Clue

Look closely at the photograph on page 144. What kind of animal is living in the hole in the plant? Does the plant look something like the plant on page 147? In the cool evening this animal comes out of its home to find food.

## Projects

1. Make a pond in an aquarium or large glass tank. Use library references to find out what you need. Watch the fish, snails, and plants in your aquarium every day for several weeks. Try to find out how each organism is adapted to the aquarium.

2. A few kinds of organisms, such as salmon, steelhead trout, and salt marsh grass, can live in both fresh and salt water. Look in an encyclopedia or in library books to find out what adaptations these organisms need to live in fresh and salt water.

3. Collect a bucket of pond water. Use a nylon stocking or very fine strainer to collect organisms from the pond water. Put any small animals you catch into a second bucket with some water. Look at a drop of pond water with a hand lens or microscope. Use a reference book to find out what organisms you caught.

## Books About Science

*Exploring the Great Swamp* by George Laycock. McKay, 1978. Learn the facts and legends about some large swamps of the world.

*The Gentle Desert* by Lawrence Pringle. Macmillan, 1977. Find out about the plants and animals that live in the North American desert.

*The Mysterious Undersea World* by Jan Leslie Cook. National Geographic Society (Books for World Explorers), 1980. What kinds of plants and animals live beneath the ocean, and how do scientists learn about them?

# Unit Test

## True or False

Number your paper from 1–5. Next to each number, write *true* if the sentence is correct and *false* if the sentence is incorrect. Make each false statement true by changing the underlined word or words and writing the correct word or words on your paper.

1. Most desert animals are active in the daytime.

2. A plant that lives for more than one year is an annual.

3. Fat, fur, and feathers help keep an animal's body the same temperature all the time.

4. Few organisms live in the wetlands.

5. Tadpoles live in the water and have gills.

## Complete the Sentences

Number your paper from 6–10. Read each clue. Next to each number, write the missing word or words that complete the sentence.

6. Many cactus plants live in hot, dry deserts. They take in water when it rains. During dry times, cactus plants use the water stored in their ▒▒▒ .

7. An area in the northern parts of North America, Europe, and Asia has a cold, dry climate. The temperature is below freezing much of the time. This area is the ▒▒▒ .

8. In the winter, a woodchuck lives on fat stored in its body. The temperature of its body drops greatly. When this happens, the woodchuck is ▒▒▒ .

9. A heron wades in shallow water on its long legs. It spears fish with its bill. Many herons live in ▒▒▒ .

10. Whales and dolphins live their whole lives in the ocean. But they do not have gills like fish do. They come to the surface to ▒▒▒ .

# UNIT SIX
# WORK AND ENERGY

A mechanical trash dump
where odds and ends
   come together
   to make
a mechanical brain.

Brian Todd *age 10*

# Chapter 11
# Force, Motion, and Work

The boys and girls are finishing a tug-of-war. Before the contest began, both teams were bragging that they would win. The children gripped the rope tightly. As someone yelled "Go!" both teams leaned backwards, pushed against the ground, and tugged at the rope with all their might. At first, no one seemed to move. Then, both teams moved back and forth for a few minutes. Finally, with one powerful tug, one team pulled the other team across the line.

The lessons in this chapter help you understand how you may do work every day without realizing it.

1 Observing How Things Move

2 What Makes Things Move?

3 What Is Work?

# 1 Observing How Things Move

Every day, things all around you are moving. The hands of a clock move around in circles. At school, you move your chair to sit down, and you move your pencil to write. Outside, the wind may be bending blades of grass or blowing leaves across the ground. The children in the picture move their bicycles and themselves toward home. Each one of these things moves because someone or something makes it move.

You can move an object in many ways. Place an object, such as an eraser, at one end of your desk. Try to move the object across the desk in as many ways as you can. You can touch the object if you wish. But you should also discover two ways to move the object without touching it with your body.

## Think About It

1. Describe one way you made the object move without touching it.
2. **Challenge** What kind of object would be the easiest to move across your desk? Why?

# 2 What Makes Things Move?

**force,** a push or pull.

The girl in the picture is delivering newspapers. She uses the wagon to make her job easier. But the wagon does not magically move by itself. The girl must push or pull the wagon to make it start moving.

A push or pull is a **force.** You use force when you move any object—even yourself. The girl uses force to change the wagon's speed and direction. When the wagon is still, its speed is zero meters per second. When the girl pulls the wagon, she uses a force to make its speed greater. If she pulls with more force, the wagon moves faster.

The wagon moves in the direction that the girl is pulling. When she turns left, as shown, the direction of the pull changes. The wagon will also turn left because it must follow the direction of the pull.

Baseball player uses force

Artist uses force

Weight lifter uses force

The pitcher uses force to make a baseball start moving toward home plate. The direction of the moving ball changes when a swinging bat hits it.

The weight lifter uses force to lift the barbells. He pulls up to lift them off the floor. He pushes up to move and hold the barbells above his head. The barbells move in the direction that they are pulled or pushed. What happens when the weight lifter lets go of the barbells? He no longer uses force on them. But the earth's **gravity** —a force that pulls things toward the earth—will cause the barbells to crash to the floor.

**gravity** (grav′ə tē), a force that pulls all things together.

How is the artist using force? Her fingers push and pull at the clay. The clay moves to different places and forms the figure.

## Have You Heard?

Friction causes heat. You can test this by rubbing your hands together quickly. When objects enter our atmosphere, they "rub" against the atmosphere and cause friction. Heat from this friction reaches 1,260°C. The outside of a space shuttle has special tiles to protect it from this heat.

Rough and smooth tires

# What Slows Things Down?

The ballplayer in the picture runs around third base and slides into home plate. As she slides, she rubs against the ground. Her motion slows down.

The rubbing of two objects against each other results in **friction**. The force of friction slows down motion and makes objects come to a stop. Without friction, the ballplayer would slide right across home plate into the backstop.

Rough surfaces make the amount of friction greater. Look at the picture of the tires. More friction occurs between the rough tire and the road than between the smooth, bald tire and the road.

Sometimes people want to lessen the amount of friction. An opening door may squeak because parts of the door hinge rub against each other. If you put oil on the hinge, the parts become slippery. Friction becomes less, and the door stops squeaking.

## Think About It

1. What is a force?
2. What does friction do to an object?
3. **Challenge** Which kind of tires, in the picture, do you think is safer on a car? Explain.

# Activity

## Exploring Friction

### Purpose
To compare the amounts of friction between a carton and several different surfaces.

### You Will Need
- different kinds of paperlike sheets (sandpaper, waxed paper, construction paper, and aluminum foil), each about 30 cm long and 15 cm wide
- ruler
- tape
- 2 small milk cartons
- scissors
- string (about 120 cm)
- washers

### Directions
1. Tape the ruler along the edge of your desk or table. Tape the sandpaper alongside the ruler, as in *a*.
2. Cut the tops off the milk cartons and tie them together with the string, as in *b*. Notice that you will have to make several knots in the string. Tape the string to the carton on the left so that it does not slip off.
3. Set up the cartons, like those in *c*. Place one or two washers in the carton on the table so that the carton does not move.
4. Using the ruler, record how far the carton on the table is from the edge of the table.
5. One by one, place washers into the hanging carton. Record how many washers are needed to move the carton on the table 15 cm.
6. Repeat steps 3, 4, and 5 with all the sheets. Be sure you place the carton on the table the same distance from the edge each time.

### Think About It
1. On which surface did the most friction occur?
2. **Challenge** If you quickly rubbed a stone against sandpaper and notebook paper, which paper would be warmer? Why?

a
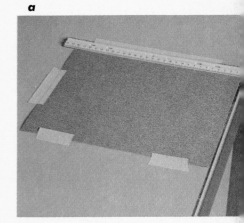

b
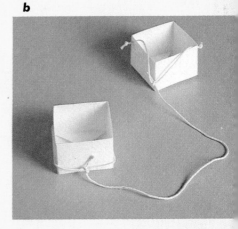

c
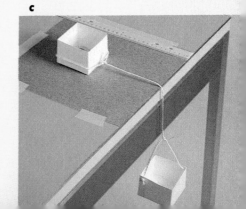

# 3 What Is Work?

**work,** an action performed when a force moves an object.

Find Out
Use an encyclopedia to find out what the word "horsepower" means.

Work means different things to different people. To some, reading and doing arithmetic problems are work. Adults may go to work every day. Picking up your clothes and putting them away can be work. Your soccer coach might say, "Work on your passes, and you can make the team."

To scientists, **work** is done when a force makes an object move. The people in the pictures are using forces. But only one person is working. The boy pushing against the wall cannot move it. Therefore, even though he is pushing with all his strength, he is not doing work. The girl pushes an empty wheelbarrow. Since she makes the wheelbarrow move, she is doing work.

No work done here

Work is being done

Work becomes greater as you use more force to move an object. Work also becomes greater as you move the object farther.

The people climbing the stairs are doing work. As they climb each stair, they use force to pull their legs up and move them to the next stair. But one girl is doing more work because she is carrying the box up the stairs. The box puts more weight on her legs. She must use more force to move the box, as well as herself, up the stairs. Each girl does more work if she climbs to the top of the staircase than if she climbs only halfway up. Think of some ways that you do work every day.

## Think About It

1. How do scientists define "work"?
2. Name two ways work becomes greater.
3. **Challenge** How would you explain to a man pushing with all his strength against a brick wall that he is not doing any work?

Girl with box does more work

187

# Do You Know?

## You Work at the Playground

Think of the last time you went to the playground. Did you use the swings and the slide? Did you play a game on a field? If so, you used forces and did a lot of work!

In a game of soccer, you use force and do work when you run, kick the ball, or block the ball with your feet.

You probably do not think of forces when you use them to have fun. What forces are used when you go down a slide? Gravity is one. This force pulls you down. But the force of friction slows your motion a little bit. How can friction be reduced on the slide?

Some large amusement parks have slides that lead into pools of water. A steady stream of water flows down the slide. This water reduces friction between your body and the slide.

What forces do the people in the picture use on the swings? To start swinging, they first push off with their feet. Then, each time they swing forward or backward, they push against the rubber seat of the swing. Gravity also helps give the people an enjoyable ride each time they swoop down toward the ground. All that swinging is a lot of work, but nobody seems to mind.

Think of the forces you use and the work you do while playing on other pieces of equipment at the playground. You probably never thought so much work could be so much fun!

Forces and work can be fun

# Tie It Together

## Sum It Up

Look at the cartoons. Write a story about what is happening, using the words *force, friction, work,* and *gravity*.

## Challenge!

1. How do you use force to write?

2. Tell how the following people use friction: tennis player, skier, person on a bicycle.

3. How might life be difficult or dangerous without friction?

4. Is an ant doing work when it moves a bread crumb? Explain your answer.

5. Whenever you play, you probably also work. Explain how this statement is true.

## Science Words

force

friction

gravity

work

# Chapter 12
# Energy Does Work

Like a wave of thunder, the cars come roaring down the speedway. The powerful engines do a lot of work as each driver tries to be the first to finish the race.

The lessons in this chapter will show you what you need to do work.

1 Observing the Last Marble

2 How Are Energy and Work Related?

3 How Does Energy Change?

# 1 Observing the Last Marble

The people in the picture spent five weeks setting up over 250,000 dominoes. Some of the dominoes went up ramps, spelled out words, and made designs. When someone knocked over the first domino, the rest fell in 53 minutes. They moved and fell over even though no one touched them.

You can make something move without touching it. Place four marbles in the groove of a book. Move the marbles together so they touch each other. Gently place your finger behind the marble at one end of the row. Now, roll another marble into the other end of the row, as shown. Remove your finger and, again, roll the marble into the row. Observe what happens to the last marble in the row.

## Think About It

1. What happened to the last marble the second time you pushed a marble into the row?
2. **Challenge** What do you think made the marble at the end of the row move?

A domino world record

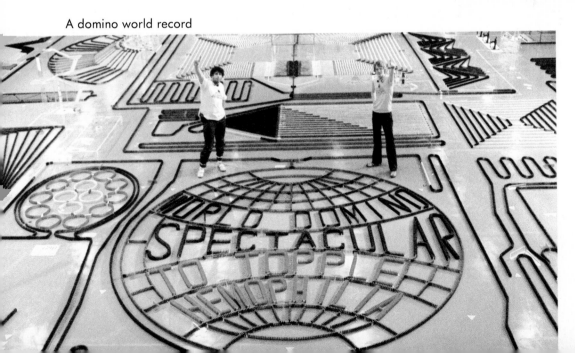

# 2 How Are Energy and Work Related?

energy (en′ər jē), ability to do work.

## Find Out

The train in the picture is from France. Use the encyclopedia and other books to find out the name of this train. What other countries have high-speed trains?

The train in the picture is racing down the track at more than 300 kilometers per hour. Because it moves over a long distance, the train is doing a lot of work.

The train moves because it has **energy**—or the ability to do work. Anything that has energy can do work. The high-speed train gets its energy from electricity. If the electricity runs out or is shut off, no more energy will be left to move the train. The train will not be able to do work.

Cars get their energy from gasoline. As a driver gives more energy to the engine, the engine parts can do more work. The car moves faster.

Athletes need energy to finish race

Examples of work and energy are all around us. In fact, right now your body is using energy and doing work. Even though you may be sitting still, your heart is pumping blood throughout your body. If you place your hand on your chest you can feel your heart working. Your heart does this work as long as you live.

Energy for our bodies to do work comes from the food we eat. You do not need a lot of food and energy just to keep your heart pumping. But the more work you do, the more energy you need. The athletes shown here will try to run over 40 kilometers. Running is a lot of work. The athletes eat balanced meals so they will have enough energy to finish the race.

The moving ship is another example of work and energy. Energy from the wind makes the ship able to move through the water. The wind's energy also moves dust, fallen leaves, and kites. Wind energy allows a kite to do work—swoop through the air!

## Find Out
How do green plants get energy to grow?

## Have You Heard?
We use the energy from gasoline to make cars do work. Gasoline is made from oil and natural gas. Oil and natural gas form from plants and animals that decayed millions of years ago.

Wind energy

Train does a lot of work

## Can Energy Be Made?

When you push a marble, it moves because it has energy. When the marble runs out of the energy you gave it, the marble stops moving. The marble does not make the energy it needs to move. Also, the marble does not destroy energy when it stops.

Energy cannot be made or destroyed. It can only change form or move to another place. You give the marble energy when you push it with your finger. If the marble hits a row of other marbles, the energy you gave it quickly passes through the row. The energy reaches the last marble and gives it the ability to move away from the row. As friction makes this marble slow down and stop, the energy turns into heat. The heat slightly warms the surface and the air around the marble. But this heat is not strong enough for you to feel.

What happens when this volleyball player hits the ball? She gives some of her energy to the ball. This energy moves the ball over the net.

### Think About It

1. What is energy?
2. How does energy get from a person's finger to the last marble in a row of marbles?
3. **Challenge** Explain how you use energy to do work when you hit a ball with a bat.

# Discover!

## The Train That Floats

"All aboard the train that floats!" Someday, you may be hearing the train conductor call out that message. Right now, people are testing a train that moves without touching a track. This picture shows what the train might look like.

Many problems had to be solved in designing this high-speed train of the future. Some of these problems are caused by the force of friction. As a train moves, it pushes through the air in front of it. Friction between the air and the train slows the train down. Some train engines are shaped like a box. They cause a lot of friction as they move through the air in front of them.

The nose on the train shown here is smooth and sleek. This shape causes less friction, so less energy is needed for the train to move at high speeds.

Some friction also exists between the steel wheels and the track. If a train did not have to ride on wheels, it could go much faster. Also, less energy would be needed to make the train move. Scientists have discovered ways to make a train move without wheels! The train still travels along a track. But it moves above the track instead of on it! The train can be held above the track by using magnets.

You might have noticed that magnets push against each other when they are held a certain way. Powerful magnets can be put into the bottom of a train and into the track. The magnets push against each other with enough force to hold the train a few centimeters above the track. Then, only a small amount of energy is needed to move the train.

The train might be held above the track in another way. Huge fans in the bottom of the train can make a cushion of moving air. A train can glide along the layer of air, using little energy.

Learning how to make a train ride on a layer of air is an important discovery. We can save a lot of energy. Perhaps a "floating train" will come whizzing through your town one day.

**Train does not touch track**

# 3 How Does Energy Change?

**kinetic** (ki net′ik) **energy,** energy of motion.

**potential** (pə ten′shəl) **energy,** stored energy.

The wooden airplane shown here has energy as it glides through the air. But the plane has energy even when the boy holds it in his hands.

The gliding plane has energy of motion—or **kinetic energy.** A speeding jet and a crawling baby also have kinetic energy. But something does not have to move to have energy.

The rubber band on the plane is tightly wound. The boy used kinetic energy to twirl the propeller with his finger and to wind the rubber band. This energy is stored in the plane's rubber band. Stored energy is **potential energy.** When the boy lets the plane go, the rubber band unwinds. As its unwinds, the potential energy changes into kinetic energy, and the plane soars.

Some potential energy

A lot of potential energy

A lot of kinetic energy

The diver in the picture used kinetic energy to jump high into the air. But, as he rose higher and higher he gained more and more *potential* energy. He has a lot of potential energy at the top of his dive, as shown. As he falls toward the water, this potential energy turns into kinetic energy. By the time he reaches the water, all the potential energy he gained while rising in the air has become kinetic energy. What happens to all this kinetic energy? It spreads out through the water, causing waves and a big splash.

## Think About It

1. How is potential energy different from kinetic energy?
2. **Challenge** Suppose a book falls off a shelf but is caught before it reaches the floor. Has it used all the potential energy it had while on the shelf? Explain your answer.

## Have You Heard?

Besides a splash and waves, the diver's kinetic energy heats the water a little bit. Also, like the rolling marble, some of the diver's energy slightly heats the air during the dive.

# Activity

## Observing Potential and Kinetic Energy

### Purpose
To measure the work done by a marble when it is given different amounts of energy.

### You Will Need
• small milk carton
• scissors
• book
• ruler
• marble

### Directions
1. Cut the top and one side off the milk carton, as shown.
2. Open a book toward the middle and hold the top end 1 cm above the table, as in the picture.
3. Place the carton 10 cm from the bottom end of the book.
4. Let the marble roll down the groove of the book into the carton.
5. With the ruler, measure and record the distance the carton moves along the table top.
6. Raise the top of the book 2 cm above the table and repeat steps 4 and 5.
7. Repeat steps 4 and 5, raising the top of the book 5 cm and 8 cm above the table.

### Think About It
1. What work did the marble do in this activity?
2. What happened to the marble's potential energy as you raised the book?
3. Was the marble able to do more work or less work as its potential energy became greater?
4. **Challenge** As the marble rolls down the book, when does the potential energy the marble had at the top become kinetic energy?

# Tie It Together

## Sum It Up

Write two or three sentences to describe what is happening in each picture below. Use the words under the picture in your sentences.

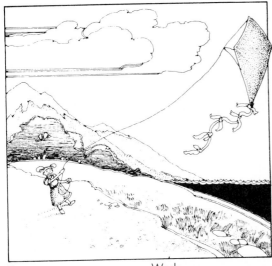

Energy         Work

Potential energy    Kinetic energy

## Challenge!

1. Why do you think people who do not eat breakfast often feel too tired to work in the middle of the morning?

2. Where do the following things get their energy to move: car, pinwheel, electric knife?

3. Suppose you throw a ball high in the air. When will the potential energy of the ball be greatest?

4. Which has more potential energy: an eraser on your desk or an eraser held near the ceiling? Explain your answer.

## Science Words

energy

kinetic energy

potential energy

# Chapter 13
# How We Use Machines

We depend on many machines to help us do work. We also use machines to have fun. The playground slide shown here is a machine. You probably use many other machines every day.

The lessons in this chapter show you how machines can help you do jobs.

1 Inventing a Machine
2 What Are Simple Machines?
3 What Are Compound Machines?

# 1 Inventing a Machine

We use many machines—from the zipper to the computer—every day. People invent machines to do a certain job faster, more easily, or better. The invention shown here looks very unusual. It has many parts. Starting with number 1, follow the steps of this invention and find out what job it does.

You, too, can invent a machine to do a certain job. Choose a task, such as feeding goldfish, opening a door, or awakening someone. Then, plan and draw a machine that will perform the task. Your machine can have as many parts and steps as you wish. Be sure to show all the steps. Use materials from home or from the classroom to build your machine. Try it out and see if it works!

## Think About It

1. Describe your invention and what it does.
2. **Challenge** Do you think the invention in the picture is very useful? Why or why not?

An unusual machine

# 2 What Are Simple Machines?

Cars, lawn mowers, and tractors are all machines. But they all need motors or engines to work properly. You use a lot of other machines that do not need motors or engines.

A **simple machine** is a tool that makes our jobs easier. A simple machine has very few parts. The seesaw in the picture is a simple machine called a **lever.** This machine is a stiff bar or board that is supported at a point. The point is the **fulcrum.** The metal stand is the seesaw's fulcrum. When someone pushes down on one end of the board, the whole board moves on the fulcrum. The other end rises.

The fulcum is not always in the middle of a lever. The boy is using a lever whose fulcrum is toward one end. He pushes down on one end of the lever. It moves on its fulcrum and lifts the heavy rock. Without the lever, he could not move the rock.

Fulcrum

Fulcrum

Inclined plane

Wedge "splits" water

One of the simplest machines of all is an **inclined plane.** This machine is a flat surface with one end higher than the other. A ramp is an inclined plane. The person in the picture is using an inclined plane to enter the building.

Another simple machine is a **wedge.** We use a wedge to cut or split something. The head of an axe is a wedge. The wedge pushes the wood apart on either side of the axe and splits a log. A chisel is another example of a wedge. A knife blade is a very thin wedge. Notice how the front part—or bow (bou)—of a boat forms a wedge. The bow pushes the water away from either side of the boat.

**inclined** (in klīnd′) **plane,** simple machine that is a flat surface with one end higher than the other.

**wedge** (wej), simple machine used to cut or split something.

## Have You Heard?

A nail is a wedge. As the point of a nail is forced into a piece of wood, it pushes the wood apart.

## What Are Some Other Simple Machines?

A **screw** is a simple machine that can be used to hold things together. A screw is really an inclined plane wrapped around a rod. Notice how a piece of paper shaped like an inclined plane wraps around a pencil. The colored edge of the inclined plane forms the ridges of the screw.

You often use screws to hold two pieces of wood or metal together. You also use a screw when you open or close a jar of peanut butter. The lid of the jar is a large, flat screw. Ridges inside the lid are screw threads that hold the lid to the jar.

Screws are used for another purpose too. The stairway shown here is a kind of large screw. A straight stairway would be very steep and hard to climb. The curved stairway is longer but easier to climb.

The picture below shows a captain's wheel on a ship. The wheel is connected to a rod called an axle. The **wheel and axle** is a simple machine that helps steer the ship.

A screw you climb

Wheel and axle

Two movable pulleys

**pulley** (pŭl′ē), simple machine made of a wheel, usually with a grooved rim, that holds a rope.

A doorknob is a wheel. It connects to an axle that fits through the door. When you turn the wheel, the axle turns. The axle moves another part that opens the door. If the wheel falls off, you can still turn the axle. But it takes more force to turn just the axle than to turn the wheel.

In order to raise the flag by your school, someone probably uses a simple machine called a **pulley.** A pulley is a wheel, usually with a grooved rim, that holds a rope, as shown. A pulley is at the top of a flagpole. When someone pulls down on one end of the rope, the flag rises. Without a pulley, a person would have to climb the flagpole and pull the flag up.

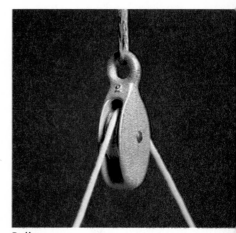
Pulley

Only one pulley is needed to raise the flag. This pulley stays in one place and is called a fixed pulley. The window washers shown here use two pulleys to raise themselves. As they move up the side of the building, the pulleys also move. The load is easier to lift using movable pulleys than using fixed pulleys.

## Think About It

1. List the six simple machines and state one way each machine makes a job easier.
2. **Challenge** What simple machine do you use when you turn a radio dial?

# Activity

## Working with Pulleys

**Purpose**
To find out how pulleys work.

**You Will Need**
- thread spool (large)
- heavy string (about 2 m long)
- pencil that fits easily through spool hole
- pail or shopping bag with handle
- heavy objects, such as books
- ruler

**Directions**
1. Place the pencil through the spool hole. The spool should turn easily on the pencil.
2. Tie one end of the string to the pail handle. Put a book in the pail to make it heavier.
3. Ask a classmate to hold the ends of the pencil, as shown. Place the string over the spool. You have made a fixed pulley!
4. Pull down on the other end of the string and lift the pail up to the spool. Measure the distance you had to pull the string.
5. You will now make two pulleys. Untie the string from the pail.
6. Tie one end of the string around the spool.
7. Bring the other end through the handle of the pail and around the spool, as shown. The spool is still the fixed pulley. But you also have a movable pulley where the string wraps around the pail handle.
8. Pull on your end of the string until the pail reaches the spool.
9. Measure how far you had to pull the string.

**Think About It**
1. Was it easier to lift the pail using just the fixed pulley or the fixed and movable pulleys?
2. How far did you have to pull the string using the one pulley? The two pulleys?
3. **Challenge** If the pulleys in this activity were wheels with grooved rims, why would the pail be even easier to lift?

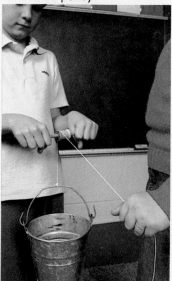
One fixed pulley

Two pulleys

# Do You Know?

## What Are Sports Machines?

Golfer uses a lever

How many sports machines do you own? That may sound like a strange question. When you hear the word *machine,* you might think of a factory. But machines are used in play too. Here are some ways we use machines in sports.

The golfer is using a lever to hit the ball. The fulcrum of this lever is at one end. The force used by the player is near the fulcrum. Work is done on the ball at the other end. What lever does a baseball player use?

A wedge is sometimes found in unexpected places. Have you ever looked closely at a figure-skate blade? The skate blade has two wedges. One wedge digs into the ice and makes a narrow track for the skater to travel on.

You can find a wheel and axle in many places. Bicycle wheels are wheels and axles. The pedals

Skater uses wedges

also form a wheel and axle. When you ride the bicycle, you turn the pedals in a circle and form the shape of a wheel. The pedals' axle turns the gear that moves the chain. The chain then turns another gear that makes the rear wheel turn.

Much of the equipment you use in sports is actually simple machines. But do not say to the salesperson at the sports shop that you would like to buy a baseball sport machine. You might get a strange look.

# 3 What Are Compound Machines?

**compound** (kom′pound) **machine**, two or more simple machines put together.

**gear** (gir), wheel with teeth that fit between the teeth of another wheel.

## Find Out

Use a dictionary or an encyclopedia to find out the difference between a compound machine and a complex machine.

Many machines, such as a pencil sharpener, have several parts. But suppose you took the sharpener apart. You would see that the pencil sharpener is made of many simple machines put together.

A **compound machine** is two or more simple machines put together. Look at the inside of the pencil sharpener. Find the wedges, screws, and wheels and axles. When you turn the handle, you make the outline of a wheel. The wheel's axle is connected to **gears**—or wheels with teeth. The gears move the wedges that sharpen the pencil. Screws hold the parts of the sharpener together.

Many machines that you use are compound machines. Even a pair of scissors is a compound machine. A scissors is made of two levers, as shown. Each lever is shaped into a wedge. The fulcrum is the screw that holds the two levers together.

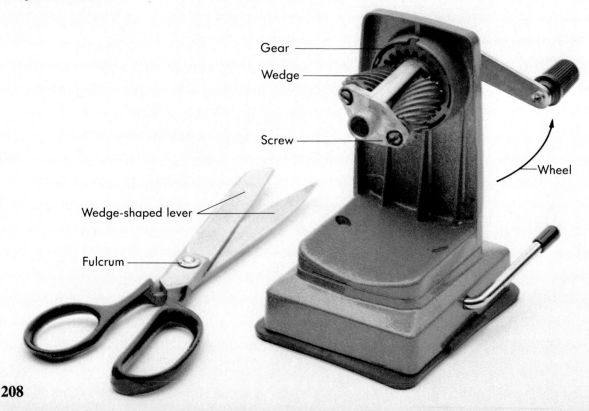

Gear

Wedge

Screw

Wheel

Wedge-shaped lever

Fulcrum

The compound machine shown above is a game.
Many simple machines work together to drop the
cage and catch the mouse. See if you can pick out
some of the simple machines.

## How Does Friction Affect Machines?

Machines help make our jobs easier. But sometimes they break down. Friction is one reason machines break down.

Most machines have many moving parts. As these parts rub against each other, friction becomes greater. Friction wears down the machine parts, and some may have to be replaced.

Friction also causes moving parts of a machine to become hot. A powerful machine, such as a car engine, has a lot of parts rubbing against each other. The engine may overheat.

Oil reduces friction in a machine. The woman below is putting oil into her car engine. When the engine runs, the oil goes between the moving parts of the engine. The oil reduces the friction caused by machine parts rubbing against each other.

### Think About It

1. What is a compound machine?
2. How can friction damage a machine?
3. **Challenge** How could you show that oil and other liquids reduce friction?

Oil reduces friction in car

# Tie It Together

## Sum It Up

1. Tell what kind of simple machine is shown in each picture below.

a

b

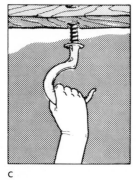

c

2. Name the two simple machines pointed out by the letters in the compound machine below.

## Challenge!

1. What part of a screwdriver is a wedge?

2. Describe how you use a screwdriver as a wheel and axle.

3. Name the simple machine used as a slide in a playground.

4. Explain how you could lift two of your classmates, using a long board and a small log.

5. Why might someone want to oil the chain on his or her bicycle?

## Science Words

compound machine

fulcrum

gear

inclined plane

lever

pulley

screw

simple machine

wedge

wheel and axle

# Laboratory

## Potential Energy, Kinetic Energy, and Work

*a*

### Purpose
To measure the amounts of work done when an object has different amounts of potential energy.

### You Will Need
- several metal washers
- string, 60 cm long
- meter stick
- small, empty milk carton
- chalk
- graph paper

### Stating the Problem
A diver at the top of a diving board has potential energy. As the diver plunges into the water, the potential energy changes to kinetic energy. A diver on a high diving board has more potential energy than a diver on a low diving board. If both divers dive into the water the same way, the diver who dove from the high diving board will plunge deeper

into the water. The diver from the high diving board has done more work. This lab will help you discover how the amount of potential energy an object has affects the amount of work the object can do.

### Investigating the Problem
1. Tie the washers to one end of the string.
2. Suspend the meter stick between 2 chairs. Attach the string to the meter stick by tying the loose end of the string around the meter stick, as shown in picture *a*. The washers should hang about 2 cm from the floor.
3. Let the washers swing gently on the string. Place the milk carton in the path of the swinging washers so that they will hit the

*b*

lower part of the milk carton. Make a chalk mark on the floor where the washers will just touch the carton, as in picture *b*.
4. Pull back the washers and the string so that the washers are 3 cm from the floor, as in picture *c*. Release the string. Measure and record how far the milk carton moved.

c

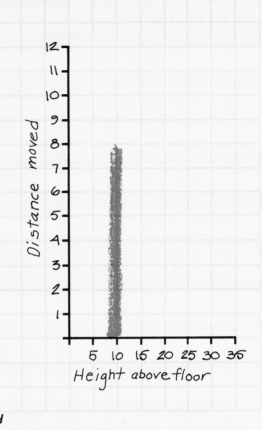

d

5. Repeat step 4, pulling the washers first 5 cm, then 10 cm, then 15 cm, and finally 20 cm above the floor. Record the distance the milk carton moves in each test.

6. Make a bar graph, using your results, as shown in picture *d*. Plot the heights of the washers from the floor along the bottom of the graph. Plot the distances the milk carton moves along the side of the graph.

**Making Conclusions**

1. What kind of energy did the washers have when you lifted the washers and held them above the floor?

2. What kind of energy did the washers have when they struck the milk carton? Was work done when the washers struck the milk carton? Explain.

3. What did you change to make the milk carton move farther? How does this change affect the amounts and kinds of energy the washers have?

4. Use your graph to predict how far the milk carton would move if you held the washers 25 cm above the floor.

5. Compare this activity to an experience you might have with a hammer. How does the height to which you raise a hammer affect the amounts and kinds of energy the hammer has? How does the hammer's height affect the amount of work the hammer can do when you swing it?

**213**

# Careers

### Building-Demolition Expert

"There is a lot more to the wrecking business than just knocking down old buildings," says Sidney. He is now a vice president with a wrecking company in Chicago, but Sidney began working 28 years ago as an engineer. "Before bringing down an old building, I would first look at its blueprints. You see, in order to tear down a building safely, you must know how it was built. If no blueprints existed, I carefully inspected the building to find out how it was built. Then I would walk through the building to see if any lumber, bricks, or other items could be saved."

Small buildings are usually wrecked by a crane with a ball. The operator knows how to hit a wall to make it fall in a certain place.

Larger buildings are taken apart by cranes from the top floor down. Often, these buildings are dynamited. Engineers put the dynamite in certain places to make the building fall properly.

"The wrecking business can be dangerous," says Sidney. "You never know what to expect when you go into an old building. But we know what to expect when we take a building down. We make sure the people who work with the dynamite are very experienced. They can take a building down without breaking a window across the street. Security guards make sure that no people are near when the dynamite is being placed.

"The best parts of my job are the excitement and the variety. I travel all over the country to check on the buildings we take down. I enjoy my job because our actions work to improve an area. We take down old buildings so that new buildings, homes, or parks can be built. I like to think that we help build better communities."

Without machines our lives would be much more difficult. But we often use machines without thinking of the ways in which they were made. It takes many people with many talents to make, operate, and repair the machines that we use.

After someone thinks of the idea for a machine, it is the job of the **engineer** to design the machine. **Electrical engineers** may work for telephone or computer companies. **Chemical engineers** may design machines that help control pollution. **Mechanical engineers** may design automobile parts or machines that are used in space. Many **civil engineers** design roads, bridges, and dams.

Students graduate from college to become engineers.

Once the plans for a machine are drawn, it is up to the **machinists** and **die makers** to help construct the necessary parts. These workers run machine tools which are used to shape metal. Some tools produce parts for radios, televisions, and washing machines. Other tools produce the machines that make furniture and other products.

When problems occur in a machine, the **mechanics** go to work. You probably think of a mechanic as someone who repairs cars. But all kinds of machines need good mechanics. A good mechanic knows everything about the machine on which he or she works. A mechanic can be thought of as a machine doctor. When a machine is not operating correctly, a mechanic tries to find the problem. Then, the mechanic must "cure the patient" and get the machine back in good running order.

Machinists, mechanics, and die makers have special skills. They learn some of these skills in high school. But many of these workers also take classes after graduating from high school.

Civil engineer

Die maker

Mechanic

# On Your Own

## Picture Clue

The photograph on the first page of this unit is a close-up of the inside of a machine. This machine is very common. It is often worn on the arm. But sometimes these machines are carried in the pockets of vests or pants.

## Projects

1. Using common objects, design and build a machine that will crack an egg, turn pages in a book, water a house plant, or some other job. Give your machine a name and write an ad that will help sell the machine.

2. Collect pictures of the six simple machines. Paste the pictures on posterboard and name each machine below the picture.

3. Choose a compound machine such as a typewriter, car jack, or hedge clippers. Describe the simple machines found in the compound machine.

## Books About Science

*The Best of Rube Goldberg* compiled by Charles Keller. Prentice-Hall, 1979. Enjoy this collection of funny inventions to perform everyday jobs.

*How to Be an Inventor* by Harvey Weiss. Crowell, 1980. Learn more about many different types of machines and their inventors. Discover how you can become an inventor.

*Robots in Fact and Fiction* by Melvin Berger. Watts, 1980. What kind of robots have people already built? What is in store for the future?

# Unit Test

## Multiple Choice

Number your paper from 1–5. Next to each number, write the letter of the word or words that best complete the statement or answer the question.

1. The force that pulls things toward the earth is
   a. friction.
   b. gravity.
   c. work.
   d. energy.

2. Work is done when you
   a. push hard against a wall.
   b. pull on an object that does not move.
   c. use force to move an object.
   d. Answers a, b, and c are correct.

3. A cliff diver standing still on a cliff has
   a. kinetic energy.
   b. potential energy.
   c. kinetic and potential energy.
   d. motion.

4. A simple machine that uses a fulcrum is a
   a. wedge.
   b. screw.
   c. pulley.
   d. lever.

5. A simple machine used to split something is a
   a. wedge.
   b. wheel and axle.
   c. inclined plane.
   d. fulcrum.

## Matching

Number your paper from 6–10. Read the description in Column I. Next to each number, write the letter of the word or words from Column II that best match the description in Column I.

**Column I**

6. simple machine that is an inclined plane wrapped around a rod

7. used to raise heavy loads

8. two or more simple machines together

9. the ability to do work

10. force that slows motion

**Column II**

a. pulley

b. compound machine

c. energy

d. friction

e. screw

# UNIT SEVEN
# FLOWERING PLANTS

A beautiful
   budding ball of fluff.
Blossoming
   blazing full with color.
Peaceful,
   quiet,
   mum's the word.

Kelly Moran *age 12*

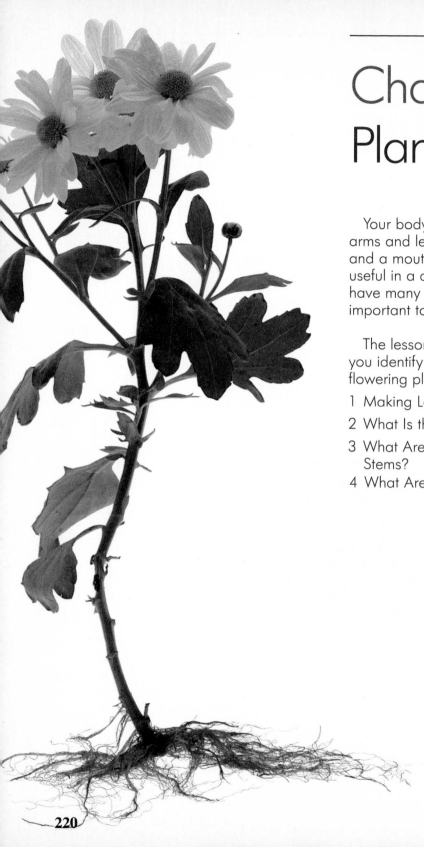

# Chapter 14
# Plant Parts

Your body has many parts. You have arms and legs, a head, eyes, a nose, and a mouth. Each part of your body is useful in a different way. Plants also have many parts. Each plant part is important to the life of the plant.

The lessons in this chapter will help you identify the different parts of a flowering plant.

1 Making Leaf Rubbings
2 What Is the Function of Leaves?
3 What Are the Functions of Roots and Stems?
4 What Are the Parts of a Flower?

# 1 Making Leaf Rubbings

Green leaves grow all around you. They have many shapes and sizes. A maple leaf is about the size and shape of your hand. Some poplar leaves are heart shaped with jagged edges. Even the long, thin blades of grass are leaves. You can compare the different shapes and sizes of leaves by making a leaf collection.

To record the shapes of your leaves, you can make leaf rubbings. First, cover your desk with newspaper. Then, lay a leaf on the newspaper with the rough side up. Place a sheet of white paper over the leaf. Rub the paper with a soft pencil.

Look at the shapes and patterns of your leaf rubbings. Look for ways they are different and ways they are alike. Compare the shapes and patterns of your rubbings with those in the pictures.

## Think About It

1. Describe the different leaf shapes you found.
2. Describe the different kinds of leaf edges you found.
3. **Challenge** Classify your leaves in two different ways, such as by shape and by size.

# 2 What Is the Function of Leaves?

**chlorophyll** (klôr′ə fil), green material in leaves and in other green parts of plants.

## Have You Heard?

The largest leaves come from the raffia palm tree. They grow as much as 15 m long and more than 2 m wide. Just 1 leaf might be longer than your classroom.

A maple leaf, a poplar leaf, and a blade of grass have different shapes. But they all have one common property. They are all green. **Chlorophyll** is the coloring matter that makes leaves green. The chlorophyll in leaves captures energy from sunlight. Green leaves use this energy to make food for the whole plant.

Animals get food by eating plants or other animals. But green plants make their own food. All the green parts of a plant can make food. However, most food is made in the leaves. To make food, leaves need chlorophyll, light, water, and air. The drawing below shows how leaves make the special sugar they use as food. Leaves get water from the soil and carbon dioxide gas from the air. When sunlight shines on a green leaf, chlorophyll in the leaf captures some of the sun's energy. This energy is needed by the leaf to change water and carbon dioxide into sugar. Leaves give off oxygen when they make sugar. Oxygen is the gas plants and animals need to stay alive. The leaves give off the oxygen into the air.

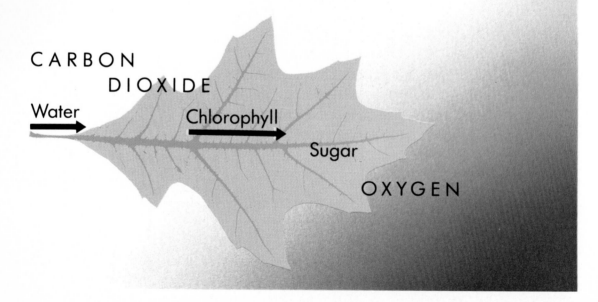

CARBON DIOXIDE
Water
Chlorophyll
Sugar
OXYGEN

Winter

Spring

You must eat food to live and grow. A plant also needs food to live and grow. The food the leaves make goes to all parts of the plant. This food changes into new roots, leaves, stems, and flowers.

Most plants store some of the food they make. The sugar made in the leaves is changed into starch. The starch is stored in the roots and stems. Plants use the stored food when they need more food than their leaves can make. The trees in the pictures lose their leaves each autumn. The trees live on their stored food through the winter until new leaves grow in the spring.

## Have You Heard?

The spines of a cactus are its leaves. Food is made in the thick, green stems.

## Think About It

1. What four things do plants need to make food?
2. What are two ways plants use the food they produce?
3. **Challenge** What might happen to a plant if all its stored food were eaten by insects?

# 3 What Are the Functions of Roots and Stems?

**root hair,** thin threadlike growth from the root of a plant that takes in water from the soil.

Radish

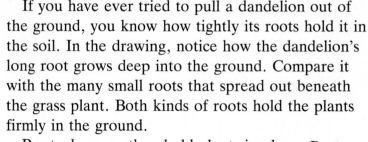

If you have ever tried to pull a dandelion out of the ground, you know how tightly its roots hold it in the soil. In the drawing, notice how the dandelion's long root grows deep into the ground. Compare it with the many small roots that spread out beneath the grass plant. Both kinds of roots hold the plants firmly in the ground.

Roots do more than hold plants in place. **Root hairs,** like those on the radish in the picture, are thin threads that grow near the tips of plant roots. The many root hairs take in water from the soil. Water moves from the root hairs into the roots. It rises from the roots into the stem and goes to every part of the plant.

Some plants store food in their roots. When the plant cannot make enough food, it uses the stored food. You are eating food stored in the roots of a plant when you eat carrots, beets, sweet potatoes, or radishes.

Morning glories

The stems of green plants support the plants and hold up leaves and flowers. Some plants, such as these morning glories, have thin, green stems. Other plants, such as trees, have thick, wooden stems. The trunk of an oak tree is its stem. It holds heavy branches and thousands of leaves.

Just as some plants store food in their roots, others store food in their stems. White potatoes are stems that grow under the ground and have stored food. Asparagus is another stem we eat.

Water and food move up and down the plant through the stem. Water moves through special tubes in the stem. Water goes from the roots to the leaves and other parts of the plant. Other tubes carry food from the leaves to the roots and other plant parts.

Notice the stringy tubes in this stalk of celery. These stringy tubes carry food and water through the celery plant. The rough lines—or **veins**—that form patterns on leaves are bundles of tubes. The tubes in the veins are connected to tubes in the plant's stem.

## Think About It

1. List two functions of roots.
2. List two functions of stems.
3. **Challenge** What might happen to a plant if its tubes were cut?

Tubes

**vein** (vān), bundle of tubes that forms the framework of a leaf and carries food and water.

## Have You Heard?

Maple syrup is made from the food that is carried through tubes in the trunk of the sugar maple tree. This stored food moves up the tree in spring.

# 4 What Are the Parts of a Flower?

Flowers grow almost everywhere on earth. Colorful flowers brighten homes, gardens, roadsides, parks, and woodlands. Beautiful flowers can even grow indoors. Notice the different ways these flowers grow. A daffodil has a single blossom on a thin stem. A snapdragon has several flowers on its tall stalk. Hundreds of honeysuckle flowers bloom on a single bush. The white flowers of the horse chestnut tree, in the drawing, look like candles among the green leaves. The blossom of a dandelion is a group of many tiny flowers. They grow so close together that they look like a single flower.

Daffodil

Honeysuckle

Dandelion

Snapdragon

Flowers can be large and bright or small and hard to see. But all flowers play an important part in the life of the plant. Seeds grow inside the flower. These seeds can grow and become new plants.

Look at the colorful **petals** on this lily. Petals are the parts of flowers that we usually notice first. Green **sepals** grow at the base of the flower. They support the petals. Before the flower blooms, the sepals protect the small, growing bud. Some flowers, such as tulips, have brightly colored sepals that look just like the petals.

**Stamens** grow inside the circle of the petals. The stamens are thin stems with knobs at the top. Yellow grains of **pollen** grow on these knobs.

The **pistil** grows at the very center of the flower. In most flowers the pistil looks like a vase with a long neck. The seeds grow inside the bottom part of the pistil. Before a seed can grow into a new plant, pollen from a stamen must land on the pistil.

**petal** (pet′l), one of the parts of a flower that is usually colored.

**sepal** (sē′pəl), leaflike part of a flower that protects the growing bud.

**stamen** (stā′mən), part of a flower that contains the pollen.

**pollen** (pol′ən), dustlike, yellowish powder produced on the stamens.

**pistil** (pis′tl), part of a flower that produces seeds.

    Look at the tiny flowers of a dandelion blossom through a hand lens. Identify the parts that you can see.

## Do All Flowers Have the Same Number of Parts?

Study the drawing of a lily. Count the petals, sepals, stamens, and pistils. Other kinds of flowers have different numbers of parts. In some flowers certain parts are missing. Some flowers of the squash plant have a pistil but no stamens. Other squash flowers on the same plant have stamens but no pistil. The seeds grow inside the flowers that have pistils. Some flowers, such as those of the willow tree, have pistils or stamens but no petals.

### Think About It

1. What is the most important function of a flower?
2. List four main parts of a flower.
3. How do the flowers of a squash plant and a willow tree differ from the flowers of a lily?
4. **Challenge** How does a squash plant produce seeds if some of its flowers have no stamens, and others have no pistils?

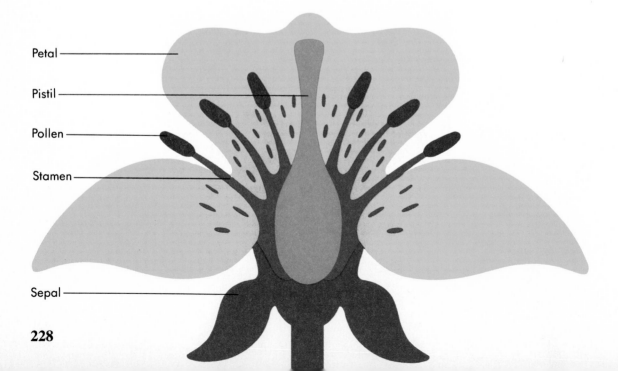

Petal

Pistil

Pollen

Stamen

Sepal

# Activity

## Observing the Parts of a Flower

**Purpose**
To identify the parts of a flower.

**You Will Need**
- sheet of newspaper
- flower
- pencil or crayons
- notebook paper
- hand lens

**Directions**
1. Spread the newspaper on your desk. Place your flower on the newspaper.
2. Draw your flower on your notebook paper. Show and label all its parts.
3. Examine and count the numbers of petals and sepals on your flower. What color are the petals? What color are the sepals?
4. Remove a stamen from your flower. Observe it with your hand lens. Find the pollen.
5. Touch the top of the pistil. Is it sticky?

6. Study the drawings of different flowers. Find the parts of the flowers in the drawings. Compare the numbers and shapes of the parts of these flowers with your flower.

**Think About It**

1. Did your flower have all the parts? If not, which parts were missing?

2. In what part of your flower will the seeds develop?
3. How is your flower like the flowers in the pictures? How is it different?
4. **Challenge** Why is the pistil's stickiness important?

# Do You Know?

## Plants Eat Animals

Animal is eaten by a plant! Does that sound like a line from a science-fiction movie? You know that animals eat plants. But did you know that some plants feed on animals? For sundews, pitcher plants, and Venus's-flytraps, insects can be a tasty dinner!

For these plants, eating insects is a way of adapting to their environments. The sundew, for example, lives in soil that has few nutrients. Most plants cannot live in this environment.

But the sundew has adapted to the environment to get the food it needs. An insect is attracted by the sweet smell and bright colors of the sundew flower. When the insect lands on the sundew's leaves, it gets stuck in a gluey liquid, as shown. Then, special cells in the sundew's leaves digest the insect.

The pitcher plant, shown here, captures insects in a different way. When insects land on the cup-shaped leaves, they slip and fall into a liquid. The inside of the leaves are covered with hairs that point downward. Insects cannot climb back up against the hairs. The liquid in the base of the leaves then digests the insects, and the plant absorbs their nutrients.

The Venus's-flytrap uses yet another method for catching insects. Each leaf of this plant is made of two halves. Each half is lined with sharp hairs. When an insect steps on only one hair, nothing happens. But when the insect steps on two or three hairs, it triggers the leaf to snap shut, as shown. The insect is trapped inside the leaf where juices digest the insect.

When it comes to insects, some plants really have a feast.

Sundew

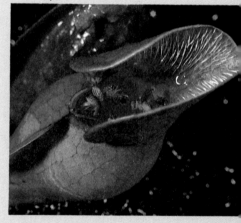
Pitcher plant

Venus's-flytrap

# Tie It Together

## Sum It Up

Look at the drawing of a plant. On a sheet of paper, write the numbers 1–9. Next to each number, write the name of the plant part shown by that number on the drawing. On your paper, write a sentence that tells what each plant part does.

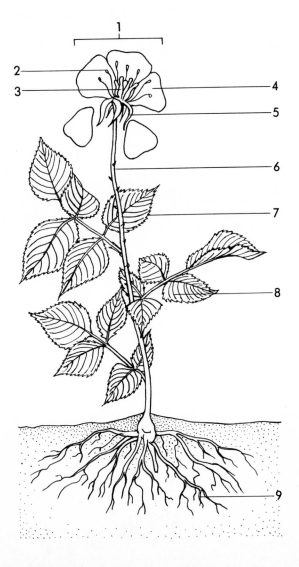

## Challenge!

1. How can you tell what part of a plant can make food?

2. What might happen to a plant that was kept in the dark?

3. What might happen if a stem had only one tube?

4. What would happen to a plant if you removed the buds as soon as they appeared?

5. How do the blossoms of a dandelion and of a lily differ?

## Science Words

chlorophyll

petal

pistil

pollen

root hair

sepal

stamen

vein

# Chapter 15

# How Flowering Plants Reproduce

If you wanted to make a garden, you might buy a packet of seeds. You would plant the seeds in the ground and water them. But no one planted this patch of flowering plants. All these plants grew without help from people.

The lessons in this chapter will show you how fruits and seeds develop, including the fruits and seeds you eat.

1 Making a Flower Bees Will Visit

2 How Is Pollen Scattered?

3 How Do Fruits and Seeds Develop?

4 How Are Seeds Scattered?

# 1 Making a Flower Bees Will Visit

On a warm summer afternoon you might see bees buzz about from one flower to another. They get sweet nectar that they make into honey. Bees also get pollen that they feed to the young in their hive. When bees fly from one flower to another, they leave behind some of the pollen they are carrying. By moving pollen from flower to flower, they help plants reproduce.

Most flowers that bees visit have purple, blue, yellow, or white petals. Bees can see these colors. They can not see the color red. Patterns on some petals guide bees to pollen and nectar. Some flowers even have places where bees can land. Find the landing place on the flower in the picture.

Make or draw a flower that a bee might visit. You can use colored paper, colored pencils, glue, and tape.

## Think About It

1. How will your flower attract a bee?
2. What do bees take when they visit flowers?
3. **Challenge** What might happen to bees if, one year, plants did not produce flowers?

# 2 How Is Pollen Scattered?

Yellow pollen grains cover the stamens on the flower in the picture. The bee brushed against the stamens when it landed on the flower. Find the pollen grains stuck to the bee's body. The bee will fly to another flower. It might brush against the sticky top of the second flower's pistil. The pollen grains from the bee's body will stick to the second flower's pistil.

**pollination** (pol′ə nā′shən), the movement of pollen to the pistils of flowers.

Before seeds can grow inside a flower, pollen must land on the sticky top of its pistil. The pollen might come from stamens on the same flower. Or it might come from stamens on another flower of the same kind. Movement of pollen from a stamen to a pistil is called **pollination.** Birds, bats, and bees pollinate many flowers. The pollen of some flowers is scattered by wind.

## What Are Wind-Pollinated Flowers Like?

Plants pollinated by wind have large amounts of tiny, light pollen grains. Many of these plants do not have petals. Petals would hide the stamens from the breeze. Some wind-pollinated flowers grow in long bunches. They hang beneath the leaves where wind can reach them.

Breezes blow pollen off the stamens. Then, the wind carries pollen grains through the air. A few grains might land on the sticky tip of a pistil. Fuzzy pistils catch pollen easily. Grasses, corn, and many trees are pollinated by wind. You may not even have noticed that these plants have flowers. Find the wind-pollinated flowers in the picture.

Have You Heard?
Grains of pollen in the air we breathe cause hay fever in some people.

## What Kinds of Flowers Do Animals Pollinate?

Animals go from flower to flower to get pollen and nectar for food. When pollen brushes off an animal's body onto a flower, it may pollinate that flower. Flowers that are pollinated by animals must first get the animals' attention.

Some flowers attract animals by their bright colors. Bees pollinate flowers that have petals of the colors bees see. Some flowers guide the bees to their nectar. Find the dark center on the flowers in the picture. Red and orange flowers attract hummingbirds. Notice how the stamens and pistils brush against the hummingbird's head as it sips nectar. Butterflies also pollinate flowers that have brightly colored petals.

Some flowers attract animals that are active at night. Moths are attracted to pale yellow or white flowers with sweet scents. Moths can find these flowers at dusk or at night. Some bats eat pollen and nectar. Flowers that attract bats do not have bright colors. Bats fly at night and cannot see colors well. They find the flowers by their scent.

## Have You Heard?
A few kinds of plants bloom under water. Waves and currents carry the pollen from flower to flower.

Stamens brush against the hummingbird's head

## Think About It

1. What is pollination?
2. What are the main ways pollen is scattered?
3. **Challenge** How is a wind-pollinated flower different from a flower pollinated by animals?

# 3 How Do Fruits and Seeds Develop?

Watch a flower for a few days. You will see that the flower lasts only a short time. Then, the petals dry and fall off. Look closely at the flower in the pictures. An insect pollinated the flower. Now, the petals are beginning to dry. The bottom of the pistil is getting larger. If you cut open the base of the flower, you might see seeds growing.

Wind, water, insects, birds, bats, and other small animals help pollinate flowers. Pollen grains from many kinds of plants may reach a flower's pistil. But seeds will grow only when pollen from the same kind of plant reaches the pistil.

Flower

Petals dry and pistil gets larger

When a pollen grain reaches the pistil of a flower, the pollen begins to form a tube. Notice in the drawing that the pollen tube goes down the long, thin part of the pistil. The tube reaches into the large bottom part of the pistil—the **ovary.** Small, beadlike **ovules** are growing inside the ovary. Each ovule contains some of the material that is needed to form a seed.

The pollen tube also contains some of the material that is needed for a seed to grow. When the material from the pollen joins with the material in the ovule, a new seed begins to grow. Without this joining—or **fertilization**—no seed would form.

**ovary** (ō′vər ē), lower part of the pistil in which seeds grow.

**ovule** (ō′vyül), the part of a plant that can develop into a seed.

**fertilization** (fėr′tl ə zā′shən), the joining of material from a pollen grain with material from an ovule to form a seed.

Seeds develop in the lower part of the pistil

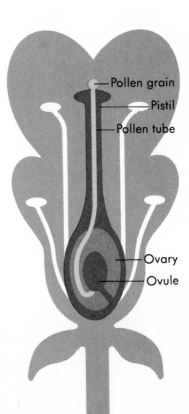

Pollen grain
Pistil
Pollen tube
Ovary
Ovule

## What Are the Parts of a Seed?

Seeds have different shapes and sizes. The seed of a coconut palm tree is about as big as a softball. Orchid (ôr′kid) seeds are so small, they float in the air like dust. No matter what the seed's size or shape, a small plant is inside the seed.

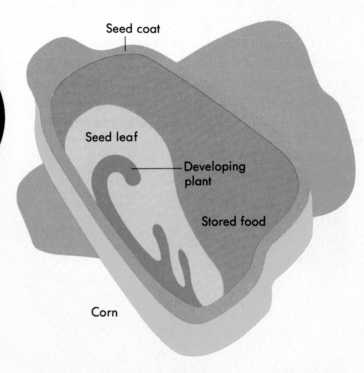

Seed coat

Developing plant

Seed leaf

Bean

Seed coat

Seed leaf

Developing plant

Stored food

Corn

The seed contains food the new plant uses when it begins to grow. A structure called a **seed leaf** grows inside the seed. A bean seed has two seed leaves. Food is stored in the seed leaves. The corn seed has only one seed leaf. Food is stored outside its seed leaf. The tiny, developing plant and its stored food are protected by a **seed coat.** The drawings show the parts of a bean and corn seed. Notice how the two seeds are similar. Notice how they are different.

## How Do Fruits Form?

After fertilization takes place, ovules grow into seeds. The ovary swells and grows into a fruit that contains the seeds. The fruit protects the seeds as they grow.

Now that the seeds are growing, the petals and stamens on the flower dry up and fall off. You can see the dried-up stamens at the end of an apple, opposite the stem.

When you cut open a fruit, you can see seeds inside. Many foods we eat are fruits. Peaches, plums, cherries, tomatoes, peppers, and cucumbers are all fruits. The pea pod is the fruit of the pea plant. The peas we eat are seeds. A walnut in its hard shell is a fruit. The nut is a seed. All the foods in the picture are fruits. Find the seeds.

### Think About It

1. What part of the plant develops into a seed? What part develops into a fruit?
2. What must happen for a plant's seeds to develop?
3. **Challenge** Some foods we call vegetables are fruits. List three fruits we call vegetables, and explain how you know they are fruits.

# Activity

## Observing Seeds

### Purpose
To identify the parts of a seed.

### You Will Need
- newspaper
- lima beans that have soaked in water overnight
- hand lens
- scissors
- notebook paper
- several other kinds of seeds

### Directions
1. Spread the newspaper on your desk. Gently remove the seed coat from a soaked lima bean.
2. Find the seed leaves. Gently and carefully separate the 2 seed leaves.
3. Look at the inside of the bean through a hand lens. Find the tiny developing plant.
4. Cut one of the seed leaves in half with your scissors. Describe the cut surface.
5. Draw a picture of your seed, showing all its parts. Label the parts of the seed in your drawing.
6. Examine other large seeds as you examined the lima bean. Compare these seeds with your bean seed.
7. Count the numbers of seed leaves in your seeds.
8. Describe the seed coats on your seeds.

### Think About It
1. What parts of the lima bean did you find?
2. How are the seeds you examined alike? How are they different?
3. **Challenge** Draw a picture of the plant you think will grow from one of your seeds.

# Discover!

## Peanuts: More Than Just a Snack

Have you ever had a peanut butter sandwich? Do you like to munch on peanuts for a snack? Peanuts are a very popular and tasty food. But you will see that a peanut is much more than just a snack.

A peanut is a fruit of the peanut plant. The peanut plant is unusual because its fruits—the peanuts—grow underground, as shown.

Until the 1900s the peanut was not a very important fruit. It was used as food for people and some farm animals, but it had no other uses. A scientist named George Washington Carver changed all that.

Dr. Carver, shown here, was born in Missouri in 1864. After graduating from college, he spent most of his life doing research in Alabama. He was especially interested in the way farmland was used in the South. Cotton and tobacco were the main crops. These plants took nutrients out of the soil. After many years, the soil did not have enough nutrients to grow healthy crops.

But Dr. Carver knew that peanut plants did something most plants could not do. They added nutrients to the soil as they grew. If people grew peanuts, the worn-out land would become rich in nutrients again! But, at that time, very few farmers grew peanuts. Dr. Carver knew what he had to do. He had to find other uses for the peanut plant so that more farmers would want to grow it.

George Washington Carver found over three hundred uses for peanut plants! He discovered they could be used in making cheese, flour, and coffee. He also found ways to use peanuts in plastics, oils, and dyes.

These and other discoveries made the peanut a plant worth growing. The soil became healthier, and peanuts became one of the country's major crops.

Dr. Carver and the peanut plant

243

# 4 How Are Seeds Scattered?

disperse (dis pėrs′), send off in all directions.

Suppose all the seeds that grow in a plant drop straight to the ground. The new plants grow near the parent plant. Soon, many plants are crowded in one place. They are so crowded that some do not get enough water or sunlight. Plants cannot grow well without enough water and sunlight. The picture shows what happens when too many seeds fall in the same place. The seeds are too crowded to grow well. If the seeds were scattered, each plant might get more water and sunlight. Wind, water, and animals help plants scatter—or **disperse**—their seeds.

Fruits with hooks stick to the fur of animals

## How Do Animals Help Disperse Seeds?

The fruits on the dog in the picture are covered with hooks or stickers. The hooks stick to the dog's fur. As the dog moves to other places, the fruits are brushed off. Fruits with hooks stick to the fur of many animals and to the feathers of birds. Some seeds that fall into mud stick to the feet and feathers of water birds. The birds carry the seeds from place to place.

When animals eat fruit, they often swallow the seeds whole. Later, the seeds pass through the animals' bodies and drop to the ground.

Find Out
A few types of plants cannot disperse their seeds. The kind of corn that farmers grow cannot grow wild. People must disperse the seeds by planting the kernels. Use the library to find out why the corn that farmers plant cannot grow wild.

## How Do Wind and Water Help Disperse Seeds?

Wind disperses the fruits and seeds of many plants. Tiny dandelion fruits, such as the ones in the picture, have bunches of fine hairs. They scatter when the winds blow. The winged maple fruits, also shown, whirl and glide away through the air.

Some fruits travel on water. The coconut fruit has a thick shell that lets the seed float on long ocean voyages. The fruits of other plants can float long distances on streams or lakes.

### Have You Heard?

Some plants have fruits that pop their seeds in all directions. When the fruit of the witch hazel dries, it explodes. The seeds shoot out as far as 15 m.

### Think About It

1. Explain why seed dispersal is important to a plant.
2. Describe four ways in which seeds are dispersed.
3. **Challenge** Design a seed that could be dispersed in more than one way.

246

# Tie It Together

## Sum It Up

1. On a sheet of paper, write the letters *a–j*. Each of the three pictures below shows something you learned in this chapter. On your paper, tell what is happening in pictures *a, b,* and *c*.

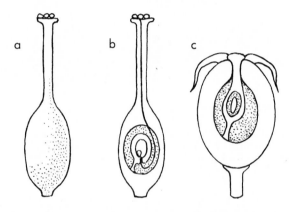

2. Next to letters *d, e,* and *f,* label the parts of the seed in the drawing below.

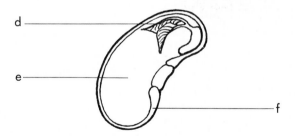

3. Next to letters *g, h,* and *i,* list the three main ways seeds are dispersed. Next to letter *j,* write a sentence telling how seed dispersal methods are like the ways pollen is dispersed.

## Challenge!

1. List two ways that wind-pollinated flowers differ from insect-pollinated flowers.

2. How do insects and flowering plants depend on each other in their life cycles?

3. What do you think happens to an ovule that is not fertilized?

4. How do people help disperse seeds?

5. How can the shape of the ovary help disperse seeds?

## Science Words

disperse

fertilization

ovary

ovule

pollination

seed coat

seed leaf

# Chapter 16
# How New Plants Grow

In the spring, tiny, green shoots push up through the dark soil of the forest. The shoots in the picture grew from seeds that stayed in the ground throughout the winter. The shoots will grow larger. They will become full-sized plants.

The lessons in this chapter help you learn how plants reproduce to form new plants.

1 Recording How Seeds Sprout

2 How Do Young Plants Grow from Seeds?

3 How Do New Plants Grow Without Seeds?

# 1 Recording How Seeds Sprout

When you plant seeds, you place them in soil. After a while you can see green shoots poke through the soil. But do you know what happened to the seeds when they were in the ground? You can observe how seeds sprout by planting them in a clear-plastic cup.

Nearly fill a clear-plastic cup with soil. Then, place some seeds next to the sides on the inside of the cup, as shown. Next, cover the seeds with soil. Water the soil, and keep it moist. Tape a piece of construction paper around the cup. Once a day, remove the paper long enough to see what is happening to your seeds. Then, count and record the number of seeds that have sprouted each day. Use a ruler to measure the heights of the young plants as they grow.

## Think About It

1. How many of your seeds sprouted?
2. **Challenge** How could you find out what would happen to your seeds if they were left in dry soil?

# 2 How Do Young Plants Grow from Seeds?

**germinate** (jėr′mə nāt), begin to grow, or develop, or sprout.

You can find bean seeds in the grocery store. Dry beans do not sprout. But if you soak them overnight or put them in damp soil, they will sprout in a few days. Seeds need the right conditions to sprout.

Most seeds need air, water, and a certain temperature before they can sprout. When conditions are right, a seed takes in water. The seed coat swells and gets soft. Notice in the picture that beans become bigger as they soak in water.

When seeds sprout—or **germinate**—the small plant inside each seed grows. A root pushes through the seed coat and grows down into the soil. A leafy shoot pushes upward.

## Have You Heard?

Seeds of the arctic tundra were found buried in the frozen ground in northwestern Canada. Scientists think the seeds were more than 10,000 years old. When some of the seeds were planted, they germinated in 2 days.

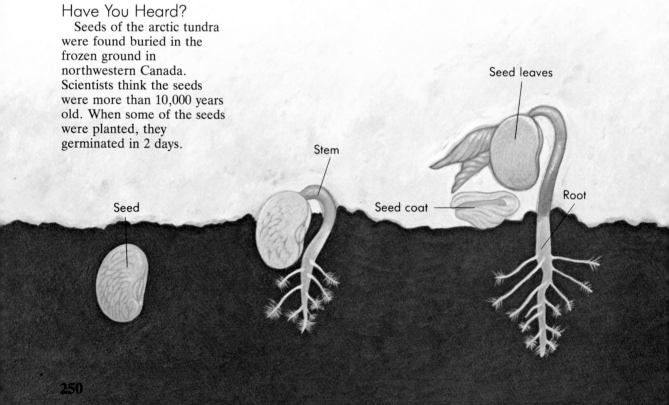

Seed

Stem

Seed leaves

Seed coat

Root

## How Does a Bean Seedling Grow?

The pictures show how a young plant—or **seedling**—grows from a bean seed. The seed takes in water from the ground. It swells, and the seed coat splits. A root grows down into the soil. The root pushes the seed up and out of the ground. Then, the seed coat drops off. Two small leaves grow up between the seed leaves. The stem grows longer and lifts the leaves upward. As the seedling grows, it uses up the stored food in the seed. The seed leaves dry up. Now, the seedling must make its own food.

**seedling** (sēd′ling), a young plant that grows from a seed.

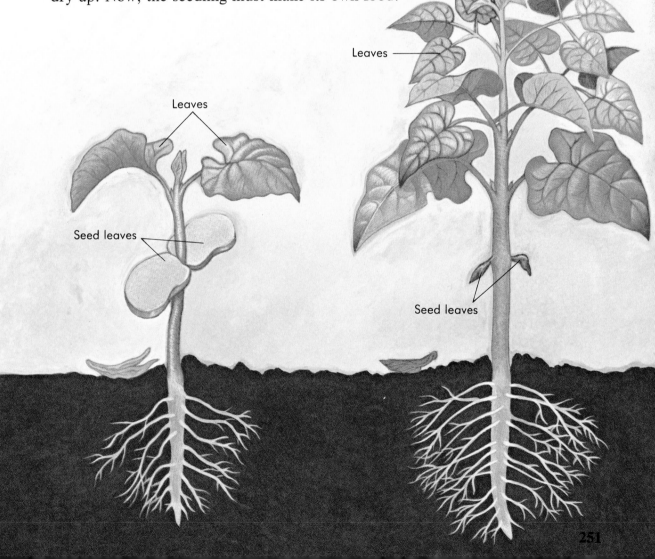

Leaves

Leaves

Seed leaves

Seed leaves

## How Does a Corn Seedling Grow?

The pictures show how a young corn plant develops. Like a bean seed, the corn seed takes in water from the soil. Its seed coat gets soft. A root breaks through the softened seed coat and grows downward. The corn seed remains in the ground. Leaves push through the softened seed coat and grow upward. A stem grows among the leaves. It will become the cornstalk. The growing plant uses the food stored in the seed. Soon, the food stored in the seed is used up. Then, the young corn plant makes its own food.

### Find Out

Soak some pea, bean, or corn seeds overnight. Put plaster of Paris in a plastic cup. Mix in water. Push the seeds about 5 mm below the surface of the plaster. Let the plaster dry. What happens to the plaster when the seeds germinate?

## Think About It

1. List three conditions that most seeds need in order to germinate.
2. Describe how a bean seed develops into a young bean plant.
3. **Challenge** Compare the development of a bean seed with the development of a corn seed. How are they alike? How are they different?

# Activity

## Comparing How Seeds Germinate in Light and Dark

**Purpose**
To find out how light affects the way seeds germinate.

**You Will Need**
- 2 sponges
- 2 saucers or large jar tops
- medicine dropper
- water
- grass seed

**Directions**
1. Place each sponge in a saucer. With the medicine dropper, add the same amount of water to moisten each sponge.
2. Count out 50 grass seeds, and spread them evenly over the first sponge. Do the same thing for the second sponge.
3. Place a sponge in the light, out of direct sunlight. Place the other sponge in a dark closet or cupboard.
4. Check your sponges every day. Keep them moist, but do not let water collect on the bottom of the saucer. Give each sponge the same amount of water. Do not move the seeds when you water them.
5. Record your observations each day. Record the dates when your seeds begin to germinate. Measure and record the heights of the stems each day. Record the date when leaves appear.
6. Record any differences in the sizes or colors of the plants on the 2 sponges.

**Think About It**
1. Did all the seeds on each sponge germinate?
2. What differences did you see between seeds sprouted in light and seeds germinated in the dark? Do seeds need light in order to germinate?
3. **Challenge** Why is it important to give each sponge the same amount of water?

# 3 How Do New Plants Grow Without Seeds?

**runner** (run′ər), thin stem that grows along the ground and produces new plants.

**bulb** (bulb), round, underground bud.

Farmers who want to grow potatoes do not plant seeds. They plant pieces of potatoes. Each piece has an eye. Notice the eyes that look like spots on the potato in the picture. The eyes are really buds that can sprout into leafy stems. A whole new potato plant can grow from a potato eye.

A potato is a special stem that grows under the ground and contains stored food. Other plants can also grow from special stems. They do not need seeds to grow. Irises have thick stems that grow just under the ground. New plants grow from buds on these stems. Strawberries send out **runners**—or thin stems that grow along the surface of the ground. Roots grow from buds on the runners. These buds grow into new plants. One plant can produce many new strawberry plants in a single season.

Onions and tulips grow from underground buds—or **bulbs.** A bulb is a short stem with thick leaves around it. Food is stored in these leaves. If you dug up a tulip in the fall, you might see new bulbs, like the ones shown, at the base of the old bulb. Gardeners separate the bulbs and put them back in the ground. Then the bulbs grow into new tulips.

Potato with eyes

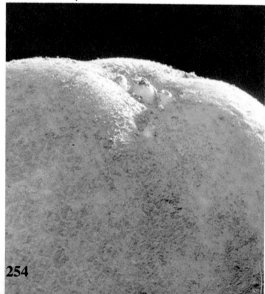

Bulb

A cutting can grow into a new plant

Sometimes a gardener grows a new plant from part of a full-grown plant. The part used to grow the new plant is called a **cutting.** The pieces of potato that farmers plant are cuttings from underground stems. Other plants can grow from a leaf, a piece of root, or a piece of stem with leaves on it, as shown in the picture.

The gardener places the cutting in water, soil, or wet sand. Roots form, followed by stems and leaves. When the cutting has strong roots, the plant can grow in a pot of soil or in a garden. New plants started from cuttings grow more quickly than plants grown from seeds.

**cutting,** small part cut from a plant, used to grow a new plant.

## Have You Heard?

Plants grown from seeds are usually not exactly like the parent plants. Plants produced without seeds are exactly like the parent.

## Think About It

1. List three ways in which plants reproduce naturally without forming seeds.
2. List three plant parts gardeners use for cuttings.
3. **Challenge** Why do you think new plants form more quickly from cuttings than from seeds?

# Do You Know?

## Some Fruits Have No Seeds

How about having a "natural wonder" for a snack—an orange? Maybe you never thought of an orange as anything very unusual. Is it really any different from other fruits you eat?

A navel orange is different because it has no seeds. You may think that seeds and fruits always go together. After all, fruits are the special packages in which seeds are stored. How can you have one without the other?

Some plants cannot make seeds. Besides oranges, there are seedless grapes and grapefruits.

People often like to eat seedless fruits. You do not have to think about eating around the seeds while you enjoy the fruit. But think of the problem that seedless plants cause for growers. How do you start a new crop of plants that do not have seeds?

Grafting is a common way to grow plants without using seeds. In grafting, a piece of one plant is attached to another plant, as shown.

A person attaches a branch from a navel-orange tree to a branch of an orange tree whose fruit has seeds. Yarn or rubber strips are wrapped around the branches to hold them in place. Wax is spread over the area where the two branches join. As the branch from the navel-orange tree grows, it will produce seedless, navel oranges. But the rest of the tree will continue to produce oranges with seeds.

The next time you eat a navel orange or a seedless, green grape, think about the special way these "natural wonders" were grown.

Grafted branches

# Tie It Together

## Sum It Up

1. The picture below shows one stage in the growth of a bean seedling. On a sheet of paper, write the letters a–e. Next to each letter, write the name of each part shown.

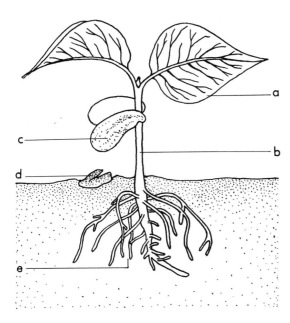

2. Draw a picture on your paper, showing one way a plant can reproduce without forming seeds. Label what you draw.

3. On your paper, draw and label three parts of a plant you could use as cuttings.

## Challenge!

1. What might happen to a bean seedling if its seed leaves fell off too soon? Explain your answer.

2. What might happen to a seed that does not have the conditions it needs to germinate?

3. Design an experiment to find out how a seed that was planted upside down would grow.

4. What do reproduction by bulbs, runners, underground stems, and cuttings have in common?

5. How does the stem inside a bulb get food before leaves develop above the ground?

## Science Words

bulb

cutting

germinate

runner

seedling

# Laboratory

## Measuring Root Growth

a

b

### Purpose
To measure and compare plant root growth in cold and warm weather.

### You Will Need
- paper towels
- 2 glass jars
- 8 radish seeds
- wax pencil
- water
- brown paper bag, bigger than the glass jars
- refrigerator
- centimeter ruler
- graph paper

### Stating the Problem
Many plants stop growing in cold weather. Their stems might stop growing taller, or their new leaves might not open. You can observe sprouting radish seeds to find out how temperature affects radish root growth. What do you predict will happen to roots grown in cold weather? Record your prediction and reasons for making it.

### Investigating the Problem
1. Fold some paper towels, and roll them into a cylinder shape, as shown in picture a.
2. Insert the paper cylinder into one of the jars. Press the cylinder against the glass, as shown in picture b.
3. Make another paper cylinder, and place it in the second jar in the same way.
4. Tear some paper towels into strips, and crumple them up. Fill both jars with the crumpled paper.

5. Insert 4 radish seeds between the outside of the paper cylinder and the glass of each jar, as shown in picture c. Evenly space the radish seeds. Add more crumpled paper, if necessary, so the seeds fit snugly in place.
6. Using a wax pencil, number the seeds 1 through 4 on the jars, as shown in picture d.
7. Wet the crumpled paper in both jars by pouring the same amount of water slowly over the paper,

258

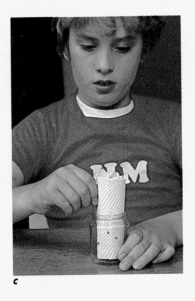

c

d

e

as shown in picture *e.* Make sure the entire paper cylinder soaks up some water. Drain off excess water.

8. Label one jar *cold,* and place it in a refrigerator. Label the other jar *warm,* and put it in a brown paper bag. Leave this jar at room temperature.

9. Observe the seeds daily for 5 days. Keep the paper wet. Each day, measure the length of the roots by placing a centimeter ruler against the glass. Determine the average root length of each group of 4 seeds by adding the root lengths you measured and dividing by 4. Keep a daily record of the average root length of the seeds that are left at room temperature and the seeds that are put in the refrigerator.

10. Use the average root lengths you recorded to make a bar graph that compares root growth in high and low temperatures over 5 days.

**Making Conclusions**

1. Why did you place the jar kept at room temperature in a brown paper bag?

2. Did all the radish seeds that were kept at the same temperature grow roots at the same rate? How do you know?

3. Why do you think you used average root lengths to make your graph?

4. Study the bar graph you made. How did temperature affect plant root growth? Was your prediction correct?

# Careers

### Horticulturist

"I have always been interested in plants," says Chris. "I first started working at this nursery when I was in high school. I just ran around the greenhouse and the fields, helping out where I could.

"In college I studied horticulture to learn about landscaping, growing trees and other plants, and improving soils."

Chris has worked in the nursery for ten years and is now the manager. She not only checks on how the plants are growing but is in charge of buying the plants.

"The best part of my job is that I can work outside," she says. "I spend a lot of time in our fields, looking over the plants with our foreman. Together we walk around to see how the plants are growing. We look for any problem signs, such as unusual coloring or curling of leaves. I also take care of some of the pruning of the trees and shrubs."

The rest of Chris's time is spent in the nursery store. She is happy to answer customers' questions about their plants. "Sometimes people have problems with bugs or fungi on their plants. Generally, they bring in a sample of the plant, such as a leaf. We try to identify the problem and to suggest a treatment."

People interested in working with plants can get jobs when they are in high school. "You do not need experience for a lot of the jobs in a nursery," says Chris. "My first job here was just watering plants. But you get to learn about plants just by being around the greenhouse. You also get a chance to talk with experienced nursery people.

"I like working with things that live and grow. I enjoy using what I learn to help others care for their plants."

Florist

Growing and caring for plants is an area that provides people with many kinds of jobs. Some people grow plants. Other jobs involve caring for and harvesting the plants.

If you wanted to give a plant or a bouquet of flowers to a friend, you would probably go to a **florist.** A florist sells flowers and arranges them in attractive ways. A florist also sells plants, which grow in a greenhouse.

You may have noticed that most florist shops do not have room for large gardens or fields. Most florists do not grow their own flowers. They depend on an **ornamental horticulturist** to plant and grow the flowers. The horticulturist measures the growth of the flowers and cares for them until they are sent to the florist.

An **orchard technician** has a similar job. But, instead of flowers, an orchard technician grows and harvests fruits, nuts, and berries. The technician often checks the trees in the orchard for signs of diseases.

Students who want to be florists, horticulturists, or orchard technicians can get these jobs with a high-school education. But graduates from a two-year college have better chances of getting these jobs.

**Foresters** work with some of the largest plants in the world. They protect and care for the trees of our forests. A forester's job includes many different kinds of work.

Foresters might make maps of forest areas and estimate the number of trees in the forest. They often lead crews that fight fires. Some foresters find lost hikers and rescue climbers.

Foresters must have knowledge in many subjects. People wanting to be foresters must graduate from college.

Ornamental horticulturist

# On Your Own

## Mystery Photograph

Look closely at the picture of a dandelion on page 226. The dandelion blossom is made of many tiny flowers that grow close together. Now, look at the picture on page 218. Notice how the pictures are alike.

## Projects

1. Find a plant to study near your school or home. Count its parts, and describe it. Draw a picture of your plant and its parts. Look at your plant every week. How does it change? How does it stay the same? Do any animals visit it? Which of the parts you studied, including fruits and seeds, can you find on your plant?

2. Make a seed collection. You can collect seeds you would normally eat and seeds from plants that grow around you. Be sure not to damage the plant when you collect a seed. Classify your seeds in as many ways as you can. Try planting some of your seeds.

3. Grow plants from cuttings. You can grow new shoots on sweet potatoes, carrots, or radishes. Stick three toothpicks around the middle of the vegetable so it can hang in a partly filled glass or jar of water. Be sure the water covers part of the vegetable. Replace the water as it evaporates. New roots and shoots will grow in a few weeks.

## Books About Science

*Eat the Fruit, Plant the Seed* by Millicent E. Selsam and Jerome Wexler. Morrow, 1980. Learn how to grow plants from seeds found inside fruits you eat.

*How Plants Grow* by Ron Wilson. Larousse, 1980. Explains the development and structure of plants across the earth.

*Seeds Pop, Stick, Glide* by Patricia Lauber. Crown, 1981. Seeds travel and are dispersed in many different ways.

*Sunflower* by Martha McKeen Welch. Dodd, Mead, and Company, 1980. The story of the life of a sunflower from seed to death.

*Watch It Grow, Watch It Change* by Joan Elma Rohn. Atheneum, 1978. Tells how plants and their stems, leaves, roots, and flowers grow.

# Unit Test

## Multiple Choice

Number your paper from 1–5. Next to each number, write the letter of the word or words that best complete the statement or answer the question.

1. To make food, plants need light, water, air, and
   a. sugar.
   b. chlorophyll.
   c. pollen.
   d. veins.

2. A pollen tube goes down the thin part of the pistil into the
   a. ovary.
   b. stamen.
   c. seed leaf.
   d. bulb.

3. Water moves from the roots to the leaves through
   a. pollen tubes.
   b. cuttings.
   c. the pistil.
   d. tubes in the stem.

4. A bean seed has stored food in its
   a. seed coat.
   b. seed leaves.
   c. stem.
   d. ovary.

5. Insects help pollinate flowers by
   a. eating the pollen.
   b. dispersing seeds.
   c. carrying pollen from one flower to another.
   d. eating the seeds.

## Matching

Number your paper from 6–10. Read the description in Column I. Next to each number write the letter of the word or words from Column II that best match the description in Column I.

**Column I**

6. part of a plant that becomes a seed

7. piece of a plant that can grow into a new plant

8. scatter

9. part of a flower on which pollen grows

10. carry pollen to the pistil of a flower

**Column II**

a. stamen

b. cutting

c. disperse

d. pollinate

e. ovary

f. ovule

# UNIT EIGHT
# POPULATIONS AND THE ENVIRONMENT

Dainty little creatures
   dressed in red and black
Pushing and crowding
   trying to reach the top.

April Barclay *age 10*

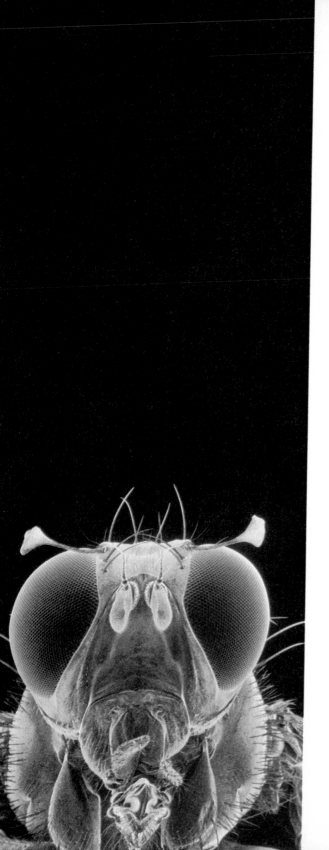

# Chapter 17
# Populations

The fruit fly in the picture can lay hundreds of eggs at a time. The eggs hatch within a day. Within two weeks, the young become adult fruit flies that lay more eggs. Some eggs do not hatch. Not all fruit flies live to have young. Many are eaten by other animals. Some cannot find enough food. If all the fruit flies from one female lived, billions of fruit flies could grow in a year.

The lessons in this chapter help you understand how many different kinds of organisms, including people, can live together in the same place.

1 Estimating Numbers of Living Things

2 What Is a Population?

3 What Makes Populations Change Size?

4 How Do Populations Affect Each Other?

# 1 Estimating Numbers of Living Things

You can count all the people in your classroom or school. Scientists sometimes count the organisms that live in a certain space. But some places are so big no one can count all the organisms there. Scientists estimate—or find out about—how many organisms there are. They count the organisms in one part of the space. Then they multiply that number by the number of parts in the space.

You can estimate the number of seals in the picture. First, guess the number of seals you think are in the picture. Then, look at the squares on the picture. Count the seals in one square. Just count heads. Next, count the number of squares. Multiply the number of seals in one square by the number of squares. The result is your estimated number of seals. Count all the seals to find the exact number.

## Think About It

1. How many seals did you estimate in the picture?
2. **Challenge** What other things could you estimate?

Find out how many seals are in the picture

# 2 What Is a Population?

Think about the number of pupils in your classroom. Once in a while, a new pupil joins the class. Sometimes someone moves away. A few pupils might not come to school for several days. But usually the number of pupils stays about the same.

The pupils in your classroom are a **population.** A population is a group of organisms of the same kind living in the same place at the same time. The school of fish in the picture is also a population.

If conditions in a place stay about the same, a population usually stays about the same size. New living things are born or start to grow. Some die or leave the area. The size of a population depends on several things, such as the amount of food, the weather, and the number of **predators.** Animals that hunt, kill, and eat other animals are predators.

A school of fish is a population

Quail

Populations of the same kind of organism living in different places are usually different sizes. Large populations of quail live in the southeastern United States. The weather is warm and the birds find plenty of food. The quail in the picture live farther north. In the North the number of birds in each group is much smaller. Cold weather and scarce food result in smaller populations. Each population in the South and in the North stays about the same size year after year.

## Think About It

1. Give two examples of populations.
2. What makes the size of a population in a certain place stay about the same?
3. **Challenge** What might make a population change size?

### Have You Heard?

More than 100 years ago, about 24 rabbits were brought from Europe to Australia. The rabbits found plenty of food and no predators. The rabbit population grew very fast. Soon millions of rabbits were eating plants. They destroyed farms in many parts of Australia.

## 3 What Makes Populations Change Size?

Suppose you live in a town with a ship-building factory. Your parents and most of your neighbors work at the factory. The ship-building company also has a factory in another town. One day, the company closes the other factory. People from that factory move to your town to work in your factory. The population of your town gets larger.

The factory closing caused your town to change size. Plant and animal populations can change size when things around them change. Populations can grow larger when they have plenty of food and few predators. More organisms can come from other places and make the population larger. Populations become smaller when food is hard to get.

The monarch butterfly caterpillar in the picture eats mostly leaves of the milkweed plant. If the milkweeds in an area died, the caterpillars would not have enough food. Some might starve. Others might move to another place.

Changes in weather also can cause a population to get smaller. If the weather is too cold when the gypsy moths are coming out of their cocoons, fewer of the adult moths will live.

Caterpillar of monarch butterfly eating a milkweed plant

Once, millions of bison lived in North America. By the early 1900s only a few thousand remained. The bison population did not change because of poor weather or too little food. The bison population became smaller because people killed almost all of them. The bison in the picture live on a prairie. The number of bison is growing because they are protected. But the population of bison is changed forever. People fenced and plowed the open prairies where the bison lived.

People make changes that affect many populations. Building homes and plowing fields take space away from plants and animals. The organisms die or move away. People cut down trees for lumber. If too many trees are cut, birds and squirrels have no place to live. Predators that eat birds, squirrels, or deer do not have enough food either.

## Think About It

1. List three things that can change the size of a population.
2. In what ways do people change populations?
3. **Challenge** How might floods change the populations of organisms in a meadow?

## Have You Heard?

In the 1800s more than a billion passenger pigeons lived in the American Midwest. Then, the forests they lived in were cut down and the land was used for farming. Millions of birds died because they lost their food and homes. People shot the rest of the birds as pests. By 1900, passenger pigeons were hard to find. The last passenger pigeon died in 1914 in the Cincinnati Zoo.

# 4 How Do Populations Affect Each Other?

community (kə myü′nə tē), all populations of organisms in a certain place.

Many different populations of organisms live together in a garden. Populations also live together on shores, on mountains, or in fields. A shore can have populations of crabs, clams, seaweeds, and gulls. A desert can have populations of cactuses, lizards, kangaroo rats, and desert foxes.

All the populations living together in one place make up a **community.** The populations in a community affect each other in many ways. In a meadow a caterpillar eats a tree leaf. A small bird might eat the caterpillar. The bird builds its nest in the tree. Then, a hawk, like the one in the picture, might eat the small bird. The organisms in one population depend on the organisms in another population for food.

Plants are the food for many kinds of animals. The tiny plankton that float on the ocean are food for many fish and other sea animals. Some animals capture and eat other animals. Still others, such as people and bears, eat both plants and animals.

Hawk attacking prey

272

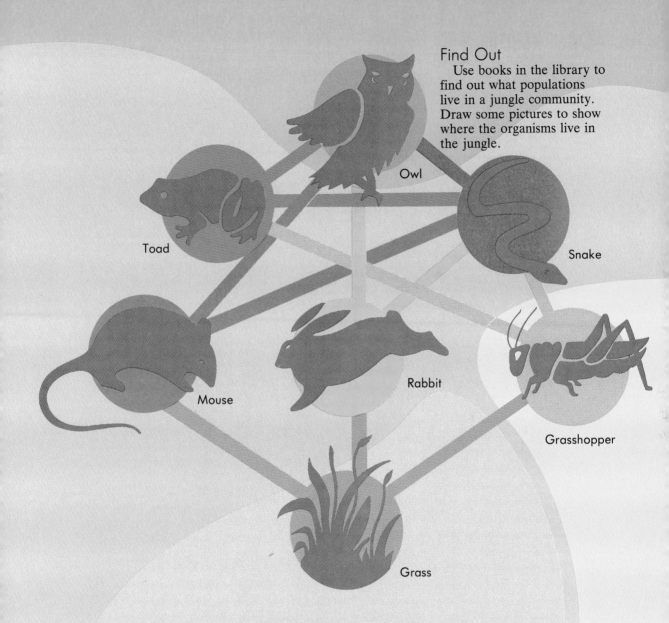

## Find Out

Use books in the library to find out what populations live in a jungle community. Draw some pictures to show where the organisms live in the jungle.

Owl

Toad

Snake

Mouse

Rabbit

Grasshopper

Grass

The picture shows how several different organisms depend on each other for food. Many animals eat more than one kind of food. Some organisms are eaten by more than one animal. Grass in a field is food for rabbits, mice, and grasshoppers. The grasshoppers are food for toads and snakes. Toads, mice, and rabbits are eaten by snakes and owls. Snakes are eaten by owls.

Plants compete for light

Plants compete for space

compete (kəm pēt′), try to get something also needed by other organisms.

## How Do Living Things Compete?

When two birds try to catch the same worm, they **compete** with each other for food. Each bird wants something they both need. Organisms in a population compete for many things. They compete for the things they need to stay alive, such as food, space, water, and light. The amounts of food, space, water, and light are limited.

Populations of organisms compete when they need the same things too. The weeds in this garden are crowding out other plants. They compete for water and for space to grow. The plants in the jungle in the picture are competing for light. Only the ones that get enough light will live. Animals compete too. They compete for food and shelter. In places like the African desert, they compete for water. People compete with the potato beetle for potatoes.

### Think About It

1. Describe the populations in a community and tell how they affect each other.
2. List three things for which populations compete.
3. **Challenge** What might happen to the grass in a field if there were no toads, snakes, or owls?

274

# Do You Know?

## Some Organisms Work Together

The Sears Tower is one of the largest objects built by people. It stands nearly 1/2 kilometer above the ground. But, compared with the Great Barrier Reef, this building seems like a one-room schoolhouse.

The Great Barrier Reef is the largest object in the world made by living organisms. It stretches 2,100 kilometers along the coast of Australia. The picture shows a part of the reef.

The reef was built over thousands of years by tiny animals called coral polyps (pol′ips). The polyps produce hard minerals from their bodies. These minerals form coral, in which the polyps live.

The Great Barrier Reef is a large community with a great number of populations. Scientists are very interested in studying

Great Barrier Reef

These animals help each other

the reef. They find a variety of populations that work together and depend on each other.

The sea anemone (ə nem′ə nē), shown here, lives in the reef. It looks like a colorful flower, but is actually a dangerous animal. Its waving fingers are tipped with poison. Other animals that come too near are trapped, killed, and eaten.

What is the beautiful damselfish doing in the middle of the anemone? The fish and the anemone are working together. The anemone gives the fish protection. No enemy of the damselfish will follow it into the anemone's waving fingers. The anemone depends on the damselfish to provide some of its food. The damselfish's bright colors attract fish and other kinds of food to the anemone. The damselfish also drops food scraps that the anemone eats.

Damselfish and anemones are two populations that have found it helpful to work together.

# Activity

## Graphing Populations

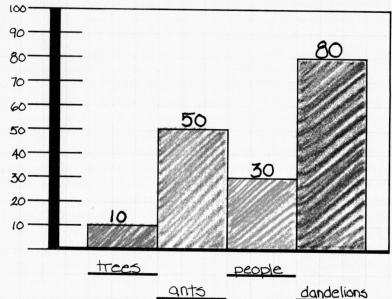

**Purpose**

To observe and graph the populations that live in an area.

**You Will Need**
- drawing paper
- crayons or colored pencils
- graph paper

**Directions**

1. Find a place where you can study the populations of living things. You might study the populations in a patch of lawn, an area of the schoolyard, or a crack in the sidewalk. You might choose to study part of the path you take to get to school.
2. Study your area for at least five minutes. Look for plants, ants and other insects, birds, spiders, and people. Identify all the populations in your area.
3. Draw a picture of your area showing the different populations.
4. Count the number of living things in each population in the area. If there are too many of some populations, you may estimate the numbers.
5. Make a graph like the one in the picture. Show the number of living things in each population in your area. Which kinds of populations are largest? Compare your graph with your classmates' graphs. Which kinds of places have the most living things?

**Think About It**

1. How many different populations are in your area? How many organisms are in each population? Which population is largest? Which is smallest?
2. Tell how each population in your area affects the others. Do some populations eat others? Do some populations provide shelter for others?
3. **Challenge** What might happen to the area if the largest population disappeared?

# Tie It Together

## Sum It Up

The drawing below shows the way populations in a pond community depend on each other. On a sheet of paper, write the numbers 1 to 5. Use the information in the picture to answer the following questions.

1. Name the populations shown.
2. Which populations eat the same food?
3. What would happen to the community if the plants died?
4. What would happen to the community if the pond dried up? What else could affect the size of the populations in the community?
5. What could happen to the size of the fish population if many people fished in the pond?

## Challenge!

1. Explain why populations in different areas are different sizes.
2. How might the size of a population change if the weather were unusually cold? Why do you think so?
3. Name some ways people have changed plant and animal populations where you live.
4. What might happen to a community if a new kind of predator began to live there?
5. What might happen to the population of caterpillars if the population of birds grew larger?

## Science Words

community

compete

population

predator

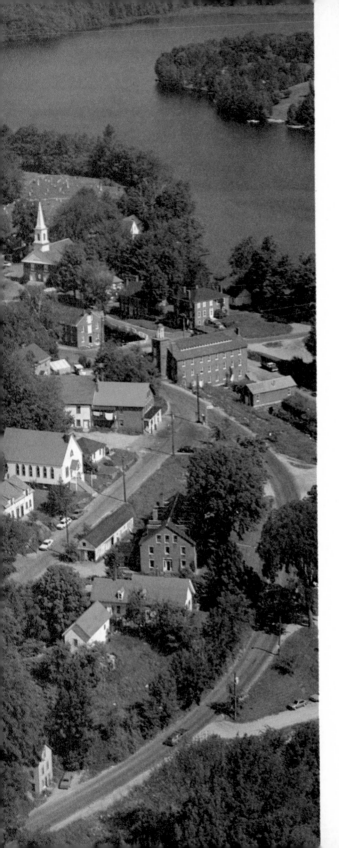

# Chapter 18
# Living Things and the Environment

The picture shows how one small town looks from the air. Many people live and work here. Many populations of organisms live here too. Notice the trees and other plants. Birds and squirrels live in the trees. Insects and spiders make their homes among the plants. Fish swim in the stream. Each living thing has its own part in the community.

The lessons in this chapter help you discover how organisms depend on other organisms to live.

1 Planning What You Need to Settle Planet S

2 What Is an Environment?

3 What Are Habitats and Niches?

4 How Do Environments Change?

# 1 Planning What You Need to Settle Planet S

Pretend your class has been chosen to build a town on small, newly discovered Planet S. The planet has no plants, animals, or other living things. You must bring them all with you.

The imaginary Planet S has an atmosphere much like the earth's. The climate is like the climate where you live now. The planet gets light from a star like our sun. A pond near where you will live has clean water. But the planet's surface is rock and sand. It has no rich, black soil. The picture shows what your part of the imaginary planet looks like.

Think about what you need to live now. Then decide what you will need to live on Planet S. First, list the ten most important living things you decide to bring. Then, draw a picture of how your town on Planet S will look.

## Think About It

1. What are the three most important living things you will take?
2. How will you get food on Planet S?
3. **Challenge** What nonliving things would you take?

# 2 What Is an Environment?

**environment**
(en vī′rən mənt), all living and nonliving things that affect an organism.

What is your neighborhood like? Think about some of the living things there. Think about some of the nonliving things. How is your neighborhood like the town you planned for Planet S? How is it different?

All the living and nonliving things around you make up your **environment.** The living things in your environment include all the plants and animals and other organisms. The nonliving parts of your environment include water, air, soil, rocks, light, and temperature.

The picture shows part of a forest environment. How many different organisms can you find? Find the soil, rocks, water, and light.

Living things depend on each other. Animals depend on plants and other animals for food. Many plants depend on animals for pollination and to scatter seeds.

Living things depend on nonliving things too. Plants need light, air, soil, and water to live. Animals need food, air, and water. Everything in the environment affects the way an organism lives.

A forest environment

Mountain goat

Living things can change the nonliving parts of an environment. For example, living things help make soil. The soil shown below has broken bits of rocks and bits of dead plants and animals. Water and changes in weather break down rocks into soil. Certain living things help break down—or decay—bodies of dead plants and animals. Decayed plants and animals make this soil rich and black.

Nonliving things affect organisms in many ways. Some kinds of plants and animals can live only in water. Others can live only in a certain climate. This mountain goat lives high on the top of cold, rocky peaks. It could not live in the hot, sandy desert. A palm tree needs a warm, moist place to live. But the pine tree in the picture is growing in a crack in a rock on a cold, windy cliff.

## Think About It

1. List some living and nonliving parts of a forest environment. How do they depend on each other?
2. How can organisms affect nonliving parts of the environment?
3. **Challenge** What nonliving parts of the environment can be harmful to organisms?

Have You Heard?
People can change the nonliving parts of the environment. In 1900 engineers reversed the flow of the Chicago River. It now flows toward the Mississippi River instead of into Lake Michigan.

Pine tree

# 3 What Are Habitats and Niches?

You may have found that making plans to settle Planet S was not easy. You had many things to remember. Suppose you wanted fish in the pond near the town. You needed to bring populations of water plants or insects for the fish to eat.

Look closely at the pond in the picture. Fish, insects, and plants live in the pond. Some organisms in the pond are so tiny you cannot see them. All the populations living in the pond make up the pond community. Each organism in the pond has an environment. Its environment is made up of the other organisms in the community and the nonliving things in and around the pond. The water in the pond and the mud or sand at the bottom are part of the pond environment. You cannot see some parts of the environment, such as the air above the pond.

A pond community

The forest has many habitats

Notice the organisms in this forest. They do not all live in the same parts of the forest. The owl sleeps in a hollow tree. At night it flies through the forest searching for food. The part of an environment in which an organism lives is its **habitat.** The owl's habitat is the hollow tree and parts of the forest where it flies and catches food.

The forest has many habitats. Earthworms live in soil. Squirrels and owls live in trees. Some trees and small plants grow in sunny places. Other plants grow in the shade beneath trees. Vines grow up trunks of trees. You could think of an organism's habitat as the neighborhood in which it lives.

**habitat** (hab/ə tat), place where an organism grows or lives.

## Find Out

Some plants and animals live in habitats in cities and towns. Observe or use reference books to find out what animals and plants live in cities. In what habitats do they live?

Earthworm in its burrow

## What Is a Niche?

niche (nich), the part an organism plays in its environment.

Notice the earthworm in its burrow in the forest floor. If you watched an earthworm for a while, you would learn what it does. The earthworm digs its burrow by swallowing soil. It feeds on bits of leaves, seeds, and decaying organisms in the soil. The earthworm leaves tunnels in the soil as it moves. Air and water then mix into the soil. Plant roots can easily push through the soil. The earthworm has a part in the forest environment. This part is the earthworm's **niche.** The earthworm's niche is living in the soil, digging burrows, eating bits of organisms in the soil, and being eaten by birds. The niche includes where the organism lives, how it lives, and what it does.

Every living thing in a community has a niche. No two kinds of organisms have exactly the same niche. The picture shows a few of the animals that live on the plains in Africa. Several animal populations, such as giraffes and zebras, eat plants. But each population eats different plants. Giraffes usually eat tree leaves. Zebras eat mostly grass. Each animal has a different niche. They do not compete for the same food.

## What Are Some Niches in a Forest?

### Have You Heard?

Rainwater often collects in the cuplike spaces formed by the leaves of large plants. A whole community can live in this habitat. Some insects and tiny crabs spend their whole lives in this habitat. Mosquito larvae and tree frogs grow to be adults in these pools of water.

Squirrel

Animals that live in forest habitats have different niches too. The squirrel and the owl share the same habitat. They spend most of their time among the trees of the forest. But they have different niches. The squirrel in the picture eats nuts. It is active in the daytime. The owl eats mice. It is active at night. Their niches are different, even though their habitats are alike. They do not compete for food, even though they live in the same forest.

The tree and the small plants in the picture all need light, air, soil, and water. The tree needs to have its leaves in the sunlight. The small plants need less sun. They live in the shade on the forest floor. The tree and the small plants have different niches.

### Think About It

1. Define habitat.
2. Define niche.
3. **Challenge** What might happen if two different kinds of animals had the same niche?

Some plants need more sunlight than others

286

# Do You Know?

## Beavers Are Master Builders

Something has happened to this valley. Things are not the way they used to be. Trees have been cut down. The stream has been dammed. Twigs have been piled. Who has done all this work?

Your first guess might be humans. But these changes are the work of beavers!

This furry animal spends much of its life working and building. From the moment a beaver leaves its family, it has much work to do.

First, the beaver must build a dam. Sticks, leaves, and mud are used to block a stream. Notice how the beaver uses its two front teeth to get the sticks for the dam. The animal uses its large, flat tail to pack mud in place. A pond, such as the one shown, forms behind the dam. The beaver spends most of its life in or near this pond.

Notice the mound near the middle of the pond. This mound of mud and twigs is the beaver's lodge—or house. The doorway to the lodge is underwater.

After the lodge is built, the beaver can take a vacation, right? Wrong. The beaver must cut down more trees to use as food for the coming winter. If all the trees around the pond have been cut down, the beaver might build canals leading deeper into the forest.

All of this work changes the land. As trees are cut down, birds, squirrels, and other animals may have to find new homes. Animals that feed on the trees lose their food supply. The pond behind the dam floods part of the ground. Animals that used to live there have to move. But the new environment becomes a home for different kinds of birds, fish, plants, and other organisms.

Beaver dam and lodge

# 4 How Do Environments Change?

Changes take place in environments all the time. Some changes take place slowly. You are changing. You are getting older and bigger. Even if you take good care of your bicycle or books, they still get scratched and marked. Cars rust. Roads crack. Plants sprout, grow, and form flowers. Then fruits and seeds grow. Everything changes.

When one part of an environment changes, other parts change too. You can see changes in any environment. Some changes take place slowly. A deer runs through the forest. It stops to eat some grass. The deer and the grass have changed. The soil will change because the roots of the grass no longer hold it in place. The deer paws the ground and breaks off a piece of rock. The rock slides into the pond. Insects in the water will hide under the rock. The deer in the picture is eating the tips of the branches of the tree. This act will affect the way the tree grows next year.

Deer

Some changes in the environment are rapid. You might live in a part of the country where storms take place. If so, you have seen the changes high water or strong winds can cause. Water and wind can destroy animals' homes. They can break down tall trees and drown plants. In some places storms and floods take place every year.

Some changes take place only once in a while. The ground can cave in or sink. Mud slides can tear away part of a hill. A forest fire can change a whole forest environment.

In 1980 the volcano Mount St. Helens erupted. Tons of mud and ash buried every living thing on the mountain. The picture shows some of the millions of trees that were knocked down. Scientists estimate that ten million fish died. Thousands of deer, elk, bears, goats, and other animals were killed. Today, some plants, such as the plants in the picture, are growing up through the ash. Animals are returning to the mountain to live. But the nonliving part of the environment is different now. Some organisms that once lived there cannot live in the changed environment. Some trees cannot grow in the deep ash on the mountain. Some animals need these trees for homes and food, so they cannot live on the mountain.

Dead trees on Mt. St. Helens

Plants growing through ash

Use the library or talk to a long-time resident to learn how people have changed the environment in your community. How has this change affected the living things?

## How Do People Change Environments?

People change environments when they build roads, factories, homes, and farms. People drain wetlands to use the land for farming. Industries build factories along the shores of lakes or rivers. Forests are cut down for wood to build homes and to make paper. Cities and towns are built where fields and forests grew. Some cities are even built on land made by filling in shallow lakes or bays.

When people change an environment, living things are affected. Some organisms can live in other places. This raccoon learned to live in the city when its forest habitat was cut down. Coyotes wander through backyards in towns in the Southwest. Homes were built in places where coyotes had lived. People plant gardens. Insects and other organisms can live in the gardens.

Some organisms cannot live in the changed environments. Insects that lived in the forests were food for this ivory-billed woodpecker. When the forests were cut down, the woodpeckers had no food. All the ivory-billed woodpeckers died. When people drain the wetlands, the environment is greatly changed. Most plants and animals that lived in the wetlands cannot live on the drained land.

Ivory-billed woodpecker

Racoon

Some changes people make in the environment result in **pollution.** The addition of anything to the air, water, or land that makes it harmful to living things is pollution. Many streams and lakes have been polluted with wastes from homes and factories. Some kinds of wastes are poisonous to fish and other organisms that live in the water. Animals that eat these fish can become sick or die. When their bodies decay, they become part of the soil and pollute it. This pollution can harm the plants that grow in that soil and the animals that eat them.

Before people change the environment they should know how the changes will affect living things. Many states and cities have laws that control where people can build homes or factories. The laws are to protect the environment and the organisms that live there. Other laws limit fishing and hunting so that enough animals remain in the population. Forests can be protected by limiting the number of trees cut down. People can also plant trees to replace those that were cut. All these actions help keep the environment safe.

You can help protect your environment too. These students are planting trees in a place that was once a forest. Think of ways you can help keep your environment a place where plants and animals can live. Think of ways you can prevent pollution in your neighborhood.

**pollution** (pə lü′shən), anything added to the environment that harms living things.

Planting trees

## Think About It

1. Name some ways people change environments.
2. Describe a change in an environment that takes place suddenly. Describe a change that takes place over a long time.
3. **Challenge** Name some changes that took place in your environment today.

# Activity

## Recording Changes in an Environment

**Purpose**
To predict and record evidence of change in an environment.

**You Will Need**
• notebook paper
• pencil
• hand lens

**Directions**
1. Choose an environment near your home or school to study. You could study your yard or garden, your schoolyard or classroom, or the path you take to school.
2. List the changes you think will take place in the environment you chose. What changes do you think will take place in a week?
3. Study changes you see in the environment you chose. Look at the environment every day for a week. Look for signs of one thing acting on another.

Look at the living and nonliving parts of the environment.
4. Record signs of rotting and decay, rusting, cracking, wear, and growth. Use your hand lens to look at small changes and tiny organisms.
5. Write down what you think caused the changes. Record which changes were caused by living things and which changes were caused by nonliving parts of the environment.
6. Predict the changes you think will take place in the environment in the next week. What changes do you think will take place in a month? In a year? In 100 years?

**Think About It**
1. How did your predictions compare to the changes you observed in the environment?
2. Did living or nonliving things change the environment most? Why do you think so?
3. **Challenge** Which of the changes you saw might make the environment harder for organisms to live in? Explain your answer.

# Tie It Together

## Sum It Up

1. The drawings below show organisms that live in a garden community. On a sheet of paper, describe the habitat and the niche of the organisms.

2. List three nonliving parts of a garden environment. State two ways the environment might change.

Caterpillar

Bird

Grass

Tree

Squirrel

Earthworm

## Challenge!

1. Describe the living and nonliving parts of the environment in your schoolyard or in a vacant lot.

2. Explain the difference between a habitat and a niche. What is a honeybee's habitat? What is its niche?

3. How could you change your classroom, school, or neighborhood environment? What parts of these places are important to the way you live?

4. What might happen to the living things in a pond community if the pond became polluted?

5. What adaptations do plants and animals that live in cities have?

## Science Words

environment

habitat

niche

pollution

# Laboratory

## Sprouting Seeds

### Purpose
To predict the effect of detergent on seed sprouting.

### You Will Need
- 5 plastic-foam cups with covers
- marking pen
- spoon
- water
- medicine dropper
- dishwashing detergent
- paper towels
- 25 mung beans

### Stating the Problem
Waste water from homes and factories often contains detergents. These detergents sometimes flow into streams and lakes. Detergents can harm living things, such as plants, that must use water to grow. Can you predict how detergents affect the way seeds sprout and grow? Record your prediction.

a

### Investigating the Problem
1. Label the cups as shown in picture a.
2. Add 1 spoonful of water to cups A, B, C, and D.
3. Use a medicine dropper and a spoon to add detergent to the cups as follows:
   cup A—no detergent
   cup B—1 drop
   cup C—5 drops
   cup D—10 drops
   cup E—1 spoonful
4. Gently swirl the water in the cups to mix the detergent with the water, as shown in picture b.
5. Place some paper towels in each cup. Use a spoon to press down on the towel

until all parts of the towel become wet, as shown in picture *c*.

6. Add 5 mung beans to each cup. Evenly space the beans.
7. Cover the cups, and poke a small hole in each cover. Leave the cups in a warm place.
8. Observe the seeds daily, and record your observations. Record the date when each of the seeds sprouted.

**Making Conclusions**

1. What was the purpose of cup *A* in the experiment?
2. How does detergent in water affect the way seeds sprout?
3. Does the amount of detergent added to water make a difference in the way seeds sprout?
4. Was your prediction correct? Explain.

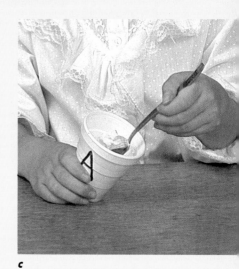

*c*

*b*

295

# Careers

## Wildlife Journalist

"I guess my career started when I was seven years old," says George. "My father was a wildlife journalist, and I always went along with him to help."

As a wildlife journalist, George writes articles about wildlife. He also takes his own pictures to go with the articles.

"I began by taking pictures, mostly of birds. When I was seven, one of my pictures won a photography contest. I continued taking pictures and sold a few to magazine and book publishers.

"I realized that my photographs would be much easier to sell if I had a story to go with them. So I studied journalism in college to improve my writing skills."

George enjoys being outside and taking photographs of animal populations in their natural habitats. "Most of my pictures and stories are of birds. There is so much beauty in birds—their movement in flight, the colors of their feathers, and the music of their songs."

George has traveled to forty countries to photograph animal populations. He is gone for two weeks to a month each time. His busiest times are in spring and fall, during the migration periods.

"My best advice to people who are interested in wildlife journalism is to start it as a hobby. Take pictures and write stories during your free time. In high school you can learn more writing skills and ways to take better pictures. Then, you might want to go to college or to a fine-arts school. In a school of journalism or photography, you can sharpen your writing skills and become a top-notch photographer. While going to school, you could start sending your pictures and stories to magazine or newspaper publishers. Slowly, you can build up a good reputation as a wildlife journalist."

Many people work together in parks, on ranges, and in cities to help keep the environment healthy.

If you have ever visited a national park, you may have seen a **park ranger** at work. Park rangers protect parks, people, and wildlife. Rangers often give tours or teach classes about their parks. They also handle emergencies, such as forest fires and first aid.

**Range managers** protect the wildlife of large grazing lands in the West. Managers keep a close watch on the land to be sure that there is enough grass for the cattle and sheep. Range managers also check plants and animals for signs of diseases.

Another protector of land is a **soil conservationist.** This person helps farmers plan better ways to use their land. He or she advises farmers how to use such methods as contour plowing and strip cropping to protect the soil.

All the jobs above require some amount of college education.

If you like fishing, you

Park ranger

might enjoy the work of a **fish-culture technician.** This person raises young fish and releases them into lakes and streams to maintain fish populations.

A person who graduates from high school can become a fish culture technician. But many of these workers also go to college.

**Ecologists** and **air-pollution inspectors** often work to protect the environment in cities. Before a factory is built, an ecologist tries to find out how the factory will affect the environment. Once the factory is built, air pollution inspectors examine the factory's smoke. They test the smoke to see that it is not

Soil conservationist

polluting the air too much. If a factory is causing too much air pollution, the inspectors suggest ways to reduce the pollution.

Ecologists and inspectors go to college for four years.

# On Your Own

## Picture Clue

Look closely at the photograph on page 264. The picture was taken in a garden. A population of small beetles has gathered on top of a flower. Later, they will fly to other flowers in the garden. Some gardeners buy these beetles and let them loose in the garden. They eat small insects that harm plants. Look at pictures in a reference book in the library to find the name of these helpful beetles.

## Projects

1. Compare the plants and animals you find in two different environments. You might observe a square of ground in a dry, sunny place. Then, observe a damp, shady place. List all the different kinds of plants and animals you find in each place. How are the nonliving parts of these environments different? What organisms live in both environments?

2. Use the library to find out how an animal population changes when the populations of organisms it eats change.

3. Plan an experiment to show how earthworms change the soil as they burrow and eat.

4. Choose a familiar animal. Find out what its habitat is. Learn about its niche. Make or draw a model of the animal and its habitat.

## Books About Science

*Animals and Their Niches* by Lawrence Pringle. Morrow, 1977. Tells how animals in a community use food and other resources.

*Dining on a Sunbeam: Food Chains and Food Webs* by Phyllis S. Busch. Four Winds Press, 1973. This classic book tells how green plants produce food from sunlight and how animals depend on plants for food.

*Small Habitats* by Lilo Hess. Scribners, 1976. Learn to build tiny habitats in a terrarium. Grow small plants and animals and see how they live as a community.

# Unit Test

## Complete the Sentences

Number your paper from 1–5. Read each clue. Next to each number, write the missing word or words that complete the sentence.

1. A group of organisms of the same kind living in a place at the same time is a ▦ .

2. Populations change size when things around them ▦ .

3. All the living and nonliving things around you make up your ▦ .

4. The addition of anything to the air, water, or land that makes it harmful to living things is called ▦ .

5. The part of a place in which an organism lives is the organism's ▦ .

## Multiple Choice

Number your paper from 6–10. Next to each number, write the letter of the word or words that best complete the statement or answer the question.

6. All the different kinds of organisms living together in one place make up
   a. a population.
   b. a community.
   c. an environment.
   d. a habitat.

7. The part an organism plays in its environment is its
   a. niche.
   b. habitat.
   c. predator.
   d. community.

8. People can make changes that affect populations when they
   a. build homes and plow fields.
   b. drain wetlands.
   c. pollute the air, land, or water.
   d. Answers a, b, and c are correct.

9. Living things compete for
   a. only food.
   b. only nonliving things in the environment.
   c. things they need to stay alive.
   d. predators.

10. A predator is
   a. the nonliving part of the environment.
   b. all the populations in a community.
   c. an animal that hunts, kills, and eats other animals.
   d. an organism that pollutes the environment.

# Glossary/Index

| a hat | i it | oi oil | ch child | ⎧ a in about |
|-------|------|--------|----------|--------------|
| ā age | ī ice | ou out | ng long | ⎪ e in taken |
| ä far | o hot | u cup | sh she | ə = ⎨ i in pencil |
| e let | ō open | ù put | th thin | ⎪ o in lemon |
| ē equal | ô order | ü rule | ŦH then | ⎩ u in circus |
| ėr term | | | zh measure | |

**absorb** (ab sôrb′), 43: take in

**acid rain,** 117

**adaptation** (ad′ap tā′shən), 149: a structure, form, or habit that helps an organism live in its surroundings

**adapt** (ə dapt′), 148: make fit to live under certain conditions

**affect** (ə fekt′), 41: cause a change

**air**
composition of, 82, 83
moisture in, 48–54, 58, 83

**air mass,** 56: large block of air with similar temperature and moisture throughout
and fronts, 58–59
and storms, 56, 59, 60–63, 64–66, 67
*See also* climate, clouds, weather

**air pressure,** 44–45, 64: weight of the air

**anemometer** (an′ə mom′ə tər), 46:
instrument that
measures wind
speed

**anemometer**

**animals**
in cold, 150, 151, 153
in desert, 149
dispersing seeds, 245
and earthquakes, 98, 99
and erosion, 126
and food, 154, 222, 272–273
life cycles of, 18–29
and seasonal changes, 154, 156
senses of, 6–7
and pollination, 236
in water, 158, 159, 160–162, 166–169
in wetlands, 164–165
*See also* behavior, organisms

**annual** (an′yü əl), 152: plant that lives only 1 year

**ants,** 11, 14

**atmosphere** (at′mə sfir), 82–83: the air surrounding the earth

**barometer** (bə rom′ə tər), 68, 70: instrument that measures air pressure

**beaver,** 287

**bees**
behavior of, 7, 10, 13
and pollination, 233–236
in societies, 14–15

**behave** (bi hāv′), 6: act toward surroundings

**behavior** (bi hā′vyər), 6: the way a living thing acts
and communication, 10–12
and instincts, 8
and response, 6–7, 8
and seasonal changes, 154, 156
and societies, 14–16
and stimuli, 6–7
*See also* animals, organisms

**birds**
and communication, 11, 12
adapted to cold, 146, 151
and life cycle, 20–21
and migration, 154
in wetlands, 164–165

**buds,** 227, 254

**bulb** (bulb), 254: round, underground bud

**burrow** (bėr′ō), 284: (n.) a hole dug in the ground by animals for refuge or shelter

**butterfly,** 8, 19, 26–27

**cactus,** 147, 148, 223

**canyon** (kan′yən), 134: narrow valley with steep sides

**carbon dioxide** (kär′bən dī ok′sīd), 117, 222: a colorless gas in the air that plants need in order to grow

**Carver, George Washington,** 243

**caterpillars,** 18, 19, 26

**chlorophyll** (klôr′ə fil), 222: green material in leaves and in other green parts of plants

**cicada** (sə kā′də), 28

**cirrus** (sir′əs) 50: high, feathery-looking clouds made of tiny pieces of ice

**climate** (klī′mit), 83, 148–155: kind of weather a place has
and animal behavior, 154

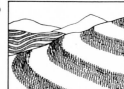

**contour plowing**

the sides of cracks in rocks
**fruits,** 238, 241, 245, 246
without seeds, 256
**fulcrum** (ful′krəm), 202, 208: point on
which a lever is supported and turns
**fur,** 151, 153, 245
**gases**
and acid, 117
in air, 44, 82, 83
carbon dioxide, 117, 222
oxygen, 117, 161, 222
and plants, 222
and water vapor, 48–49
and weathering, 117
**gear** (gir), 208: wheel with teeth that fit
between the teeth of another wheel
**germinate** (jėr′mə nāt), 250, 253: begin to
grow, or develop, or sprout
**gills,** (gilz) 161, 162, 168: part of a water
animal's body through which the animal
takes oxygen from water and gives off
carbon dioxide
**glacier** (glā′shər), 122, 130–133, 135–136: a
huge mass of ice that moves slowly and
erodes the land
**Grand Canyon,** 134
**gravity** (grav′ə tē), 183, 188: a force that
pulls all things together
**Great Barrier Reef,** 275
**Great Lakes,** 132
**Great Plains,** 134
**Great Sphinx,** 116, 121
**habitat** (hab′ə tat), 283, 287: place where
an organism grows or lives
**hail,** 53
**heat,** 63, 184, 194, 197
**hibernate** (hī′bər nāt), 154: spend the winter
in a state in which all the functions of
the body slow down greatly
**hill,** 135
**honeybees,** 13–15 *See also* bees
**hurricane,** 64–65, 67
**ice**
and erosion, 120, 122
and glaciers, 122, 130–133, 135–136
and precipitation, 53

**ice age,** 131–133: a long period of time
when much of the earth is covered by
ice
**inclined** (in klīnd′) **plane,** 203: simple
machine that is a flat surface with one
end higher than the other
**infer** (in fėr′), 129: using what you already
know to make a decision
**information** (in′fər mā′shən), 10: knowledge
given or received about some fact or
event
**insects**
behavior of, 6–8
eggs, 20, 21, 26–30
life cycles of, 24, 26–30
societies of, 14–15
**instinct** (in′stingkt), 8: act an animal does
without being taught
**kinetic** (ki net′ik) **energy,** 196–198: energy
of motion
**land**
and continents, 82–83, 88–89
and erosion, 120–126
and glaciers, 130–133, 135–136
and temperature, 43
**landform,** 134, 135–136: a feature, such as
a plain, plateau, hill, or mountain, that
gives the land its shape
**larva** (lär′və), 26: the young
of an animal
that is different in
form from the adult.
[Plural: **larvae** (lär′vē)]
**lava,** 100, 101, 102:
melted rock or magma
that comes out onto
the surface of the earth

larva

**layer** (lā′yər), 85: (n.) one thickness
**leaves**
food stored in, 222–223, 254
functions of, 160, 222–223
in seasonal changes, 152
storing water in, 147, 148
**lever** (lev′ər), 202, 208: simple machine
made of a bar that is supported at a
point and turns on that point

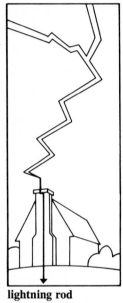

ovary

| a hat | i it | oi oil | ch child | | a in about |
|---|---|---|---|---|---|
| ā age | ī ice | ou out | ng long | | e in taken |
| ä far | o hot | u cup | sh she | ə = | i in pencil |
| e let | ō open | u̇ put | th thin | | o in lemon |
| ē equal | ô order | ü rule | ᴛʜ then | | u in circus |
| ėr term | | | zh measure | | |

changes in size of, 270–271
and communities, 272
and competition, 274
and environment, 278, 279–292
estimating, 267
*See also* community, environment

**potential** (pə ten′shəl) **energy,** 196–198: stored energy

**precipitation** (pri sip′ə tā′shən), 53, 54: moisture that falls to the ground

**predator** (pred′ə tər), 268: an animal that hunts, kills, and eats other animals

**predict** (pri dikt′), 68: tell about something before it happens

**predicting**
changes, 19, 129
earthquakes, 98, 99
weather, 68–69

**property** (prop′ər tē), 222: quality or power belonging specially to something

**pulley** (pu̇l′ē), 205–206: simple machine made of a wheel, usually with a grooved rim, that holds a rope

**pupa** (pyü′pə), 26: stage in insect life cycle between larva and adult. [Plural: **pupae** (pyü′pē)]

**queen bee,** 15: female bee that lays the eggs in a beehive

**rain,** 52–53, 54, 60, 116, 117, 124

**rain gauge** (gāj), 54: instrument that measures the depth of rainfall

**reforestation** (rē′fôr ə stā′shən), 124: the replanting of trees

**reproduce** (rē′prə düs′), 21: produce offspring

**reproducing**
animals, 18–30
plants, 227, 232–246, 250–253, 254–255

**response** (ri spons′), 6–8: activity that occurs because of a stimulus

**rocks**
and faults, 94–95
and glaciers, 130–133
and weathering, 116–118

**roots,** 152
food in, 222, 223
functions of, 224–225
and new plants, 254

**root hair,** 224: thin threadlike growth from the root of a plant that takes in water from the soil

**runner** (run′ər), 254: thin stem that grows along the ground and produces new plants

runner

**salt marsh,** 165

**saltwater** *See* ocean

**San Andreas Fault,** 95, 96

**satellite** (sat′l īt), 69: object made by people that circles a planet

**scale,** 161

**screw,** 204, 208: simple machine that is an inclined plane wrapped around a rod

**seasons,** 152–153

**seeds**
of annuals, perennials, 152
in cold, 150–151
in desert, 148–149
development of, 238–239
dispersed, 244–246
and fruits, 241, 245, 246
germinating, 250–253
growth of, 227, 228, 249, 251–252
parts of, 240, 242

**seed coat,** 240, 250: outer covering of a seed

**seed leaf,** 240: structure in the seed of a plant

**seedling** (sēd′ling), 251–252: young plant that grows from a seed

**sepal** (sē′pəl), 227: leaflike part of a flower that protects the growing bud

**simple machine,** 202–205: one of six basic tools that helps us do work

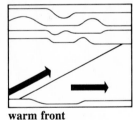

| a hat | i it | oi oil | ch child | ( a in about |
|-------|------|--------|----------|---------------|
| ā age | ī ice | ou out | ng long | e in taken |
| ä far | o hot | u cup | sh she | ə = { i in pencil |
| e let | ō open | u̇ put | th thin | o in lemon |
| ē equal | ô order | ü rule | ᵭH then | u in circus |
| ėr term | | | zh measure | |

**water vapor** (vā′pər), 48–49, 51–53, 64:
water that is in the form of gas

**waves**
in earth, 85
and erosion, 121

**weather**
air masses and fronts, 58–59
and air pressure, 44–45
balloon, 40, 68
and clouds, 49–50, 52–53
hurricanes, 64–65, 67
and population size, 269, 270
and precipitation, 52–54
predictions, 68–69
and temperature, 41–43
thunderstorms, 59, 60–63
tornadoes, 56, 66
and water vapor, 48–49, 51
*See also* air mass, climate, clouds

**weathering,** 116–119:
the breaking down of rock

**wedge** (wej), 203, 208: simple machine used
to cut or split something

**wetland** (wet′land), 164–165, 290: place
where water collects on land

**whales,** 168

**wheel and axle** (ak′səl), 204–205, 208:
simple machine made of a rod
connected to the center of a wheel

**wind**
and air pressure, 45
dispersing seeds, 244, 246
energy, 193
erosion, 120, 121, 124, 126
in hurricanes, 64–65
measuring, 46, 47
and pollination, 235
in tornadoes, 66

**wind vane**

**wind vane** (vān), 46, 68:
instrument that
measures wind direction

**work,** 180, 186–187: an action performed
when a force makes an object move
*See also* energy, force, motion

**worker bee,** 15: female bee that does the
work for a beehive

# Acknowledgments

Positions of photographs are shown in abbreviated form as follows: top **(t)**, bottom **(b)**, left **(l)**, right **(r)**, center **(c)**. All photographs not credited are the property of Scott, Foresman and Company.  Cover, illustration by William Peterson, photograph by David Muench; **2,** Jeff Foott/Bruce Coleman Ltd.; **4,** Jane Burton/Bruce Coleman Ltd.; **6,** J. L. G. Grande/Bruce Coleman Ltd.; **7,** (l) E.R. Degginger, (r) Thomas Eisner; **8,** (l) Jane Burton/Bruce Coleman Ltd., (r) David G. Allen; **10,** Ken Lucas/Seaphot; **12,** (t) Tom Brakefield/Taurus, (c) E. R. Degginger, (b) George Holton/Photo Researchers; **14,** (l) Jack Dermid, (r) Philippe Varin/Jacana; **15,** Jeff Foott/Bruce Coleman Inc.; **18,** J. L. Mason/Ardea London; **20,** Jane Burton/Bruce Coleman Ltd.; **21,** Breck P. Kent; **22,** (l) Edward S. Ross, (r) Peter Fronk; **23,** (tl)

Root-Okapia, **(tr)** Francisco Erize/Bruce Coleman Ltd., **(br)** Robert Frerck/Woodfin Camp & Assoc.; **25,** Breck P. Kent; **26,** (l) Lynn M. Stone/Bruce Coleman Ltd., (r) E. R. Degginger; **27,** E. R. Degginger; **28,** Breck P. Kent; **30,** James P. Rowan; **36,** (l) James P. Rowan, (r) Robert H. Glaze/Artstreet; **38,** NASA; **40,** Doris Gehrig Barker; **44,** Uldis Saule; **46,** (l) E. R. Degginger; **47,** Jim Brandenburg; **48,** Charles E. Schmidt/Taurus; **49,** Peter Fronk; **50,** (tl) David Herman/Shostal, (tr) A. L. Parnes/Photo Researchers, (b) E. R. Degginger; **53,** (t) National Center for Atmospheric Research, sponsored by the National Science Foundation, **(b)** NOAA; **56,** E. R. Degginger; **57,** NASA; **61,** Ray Manley/Shostal; **62,** Brown Brothers; **63,** (l) Russ Kinne/Photo Researchers, **(r)** Cary Wolinsky/Stock, Boston; **65,** (t)

Annie Griffiths, (l) Siskind/Gamma-Liaison; **66**, Joel Anderson/Shostal; **67**, (r) U.S. Air Force, (b) Clyde H. Smith/Peter Arnold, Inc.; **68**, (r) Tom Pantages; **69**, (l) NOAA Satellite Photograph, (r) NASA; **75**, U.S. Air Force; **76**, (r) Phil Degginger; **78**, Dick Rowan/Photo Researchers; **80**, John S. Shelton; **81**, David Hiser; **83**, NASA; **84**, George Hunter/Shostal; **87**, Kenneth Garrett/Woodfin Camp & Assoc.; **92**, Ed Clark/Life Magazine © 1944 Time Inc.; **95**, (l) George Hall, (r) G. K. Gilbert/U.S. Geological Survey; **96–97**, Pierre Vauthey/Sygma; **98**, Charles O'Rear/West Light; **99**, Visage-Nature Agence Photographique; **100**, (l) Maurice Krafft/Explorer, (r) John S. Shelton; **101**, Roger Werth/Woodfin Camp & Assoc.; **103**, R. Uchida/Orion Press; **109**, (t) Maurice Krafft/Explorer, (m) Jodi Cobb/Woodfin Camp, Inc.; (b) John Earle/The Stock Market; **112**, Gene Ahrens; **114**, Shostal; **116**, A. Thomas/Explorer; **117**, Harald Sund; **119**, (t) Paul Friedrich from E. R. Degginger, (b) Erik Akerblom/Kay Reese & Assoc.; **120**, (l) Bryan Allen/Shostal; **121**, (l) Harald Sund, (r) Ruth A. Cordner/Root Resources; **122**, E. R. Degginger; **124**, (l) Harald Sund, (r) Craig Aurness/West Light; **125**, Cary Wolinsky/Stock, Boston; **126**, (l) Jerome Wyckoff, (r) R. Truchot/Explorer; **128**, Martin W. Vanderwall/Leo de Wys, Inc.; **129**, (l) Robert H. Glaze/Artstreet; **130**, (l) Cary Wolinsky/After-Image, (r) Jerome Wyckoff; **131**, (l) E. R. Degginger; **132**, (r) Cary Wolinsky/Stock, Boston; **134**, (tl) Michael Collier; **135**, (tr) Horst Schapes/Peter Arnold, Inc., (br) Pat O'Hara; **140**, Robert Frerck/Odyssey Productions; **141**, (r) Pierre Kopp/West Light; **144**, Jen & Des Bartlett/Bruce Coleman, Inc.; **146**, Howard Platt/Seaphot; **148-9**, Gene Ahrens; **148**, (l) Stephen J. Krasemann/Peter Arnold, Inc.; **149**, (l) Bob & Clara Calhoun/Bruce Coleman Ltd.; **150**, Stephen J. Krasemann/DRK Photo; **151**, Leonard L. Rue/Shostal; **152**, Eric Crichton/Bruce Coleman Ltd., (r) W. H. Hodge/Peter Arnold, Inc.; **153**, (l) Phil Dotson/DPI, (r) Bob & Clara Calhoun/Bruce Coleman, Inc.; **155**, (t) Leonard Lee Rue III/Bruce Coleman, Inc., (b) Phil Dotson/DPI; **156**, Craig Aurness/West Light; **158**, Mike Mazzaschi/Stock, Boston; **159**, Alfred Owczarzak/Taurus; **160**, Jack Dermid; **161**, Breck P. Kent; **162**, Hans Pfletschinger/Peter Arnold, Inc.; **163**, Hans Reinhard/Bruce Coleman Ltd.; **164**, Sylvia Johnson/Woodfin Camp & Assoc.; **165**, Tom & Michele Grimm/After-Image; **166**, E. R. Degginger; **167**, Claude Carre/Jacana; **168**, Claude Carre/Jacana; **174**, Kent & Donna Dannen/Photo Researchers; **175**, (l) M. P. Kahl/Bruce Coleman, Inc., (r) M. Timothy O'Keefe/Tom Stack & Assoc.; **178**, Werner H. Müller/Peter Arnold, Inc.; **190**, Joseph F. Viesti; **191**, (b) National Hemophilia Foundation, World Domino Spectacular; **192–93**, (b) Document SNCF/Explorer; **192**, (t) Everett C. Johnson; **193**, (t) Chuck Place; **195**, Krauss Maffei/Bavaria-Verlag; **203**, (r) Hank Morgan/Rainbow; **204**, (l) Chuck Place, (r) Ron Boff/Alpha; **205**, (l) Craig Wells/After-Image; **214**, George Mars Cassidy/Globe Photos from Stockphotos Inc.; **215**, (tr) Salvatore Giordano III; **233**, E. R. Degginger; **224**, Jack Dermid; **226**, (tl) Breck P. Kent, (bl) E. R. Degginger; **230**, (t) E. R. Degginger, (m) Breck P. Kent, (b) E. R. Degginger; **233**, (tr) Stephen Dalton/Oxford Scientific Films Ltd. from Animals Animals; **237**, (t) Stephen Dalton/Oxford Scientific Films Ltd.; **243**, Bettmann Archive; **248**, Ed Cooper; **256**, John Kohout/Root Resources; **261**, (l) D'Arazien/Shostal, (r) Sisse Brimberg/Woodfin Camp, Inc.; **264**, Edward S. Ross; **266**, David Scharf/Peter Arnold, Inc.; **267**, Stephen J. Krasemann/Peter Arnold, Inc.; **268**, James M. Cribb; **269**, Joe Van Wormer/Bruce Coleman Ltd.; **270**, (l) Edward S. Ross; **270–71**, David R. Frazier; **272**, Manfred Danegger/Jacana; **274**, (l) Brian Parker/Tom Stack & Assoc.; **275**, (tr) Grandadam/Explorer, (br) Jeff Rotman/Peter Arnold, Inc.; **278**, Michael Philip Manheim/After-Image; **280**, Mark Wallace/Shostal; **281**, (tl) Jeff March, (tr) E. R. Degginger; **284**, John X. Sundance/Jacana; **285**, Gerald Cubitt; **286**, (l) Breck P. Kent, (br) Ed Cooper/Shostal; **287**, (b) Dane McGilliway/U.S. Fish and Wildlife Service, (l) Leonard Lee Rue III/Bruce Coleman Ltd.; **288**, Leonard Lee Rue III/Bruce Coleman Ltd.; **289**, (r) Owen Franken/Stock, Boston, (l) J. Rosenbaum/U.S. Geological Survey; **290**, (l) Tom McHugh/Photo Researchers, (r) Breck P. Kent; **291**, Jim Brandenburg; **297**, (t) David R. Frazier.

Ligature Publishing Services, Inc.: design implementation, internal art and photographic direction.

We wish to express our appreciation to the following schools for their contributions:

**Poems** for the series were written by children at Fairfield Public Schools, Fairfield, Connecticut; Greeley School, Winnetka, Illinois; Howland School, Chicago, Illinois; Indian Oasis Elementary District, Sells, Arizona; and Model Laboratory School, Eastern Kentucky University, Richmond, Kentucky.

**Cloze reading tests** for the series were administered at Banting-Elementary School, Waukesha, Wisconsin; and Gospel Lutheran Grade School, Milwaukee, Wisconsin.

**Photographs** for Book 4 were taken at Orrington School, Evanston, Illinois; and Martin Luther King Lab School, Evanston, Illinois.

# Using Metric

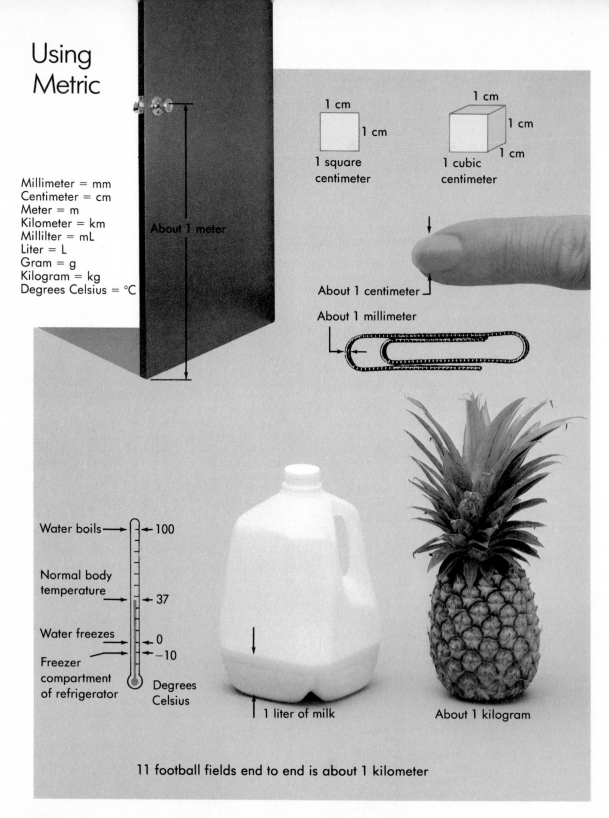

Millimeter = mm
Centimeter = cm
Meter = m
Kilometer = km
Milliliter = mL
Liter = L
Gram = g
Kilogram = kg
Degrees Celsius = °C

About 1 meter

1 cm
1 cm
1 square centimeter

1 cm
1 cm
1 cm
1 cubic centimeter

About 1 centimeter

About 1 millimeter

Water boils → 100
Normal body temperature → 37
Water freezes → 0
Freezer compartment of refrigerator → −10
Degrees Celsius

1 liter of milk

About 1 kilogram

11 football fields end to end is about 1 kilometer